Advancing College Vocabulary & Spelling Skills

Second Edition

Lawrence Scheg

184

> **This book belongs to :**
>
> Name: Yulisa A- Cardona
> Street: _____
> City: _____ State: ____
> Phone: _____
>
> **The information above is optional**

Sierra Publishing
South Lake Tahoe, California

ISBN: 0-9742756-0-3 ISBN 13: 978-0-97422756-0-4

Published by
Sierra Publishing
1034 Emerald Bay Rd. #125
South Lake Tahoe, CA 96150

Contact for Domestic and International Orders:
Send E-mail to: mailsierrapublishing@yahoo.com
or visit www.SierraPublishing.com

Printed in the United States of America

7th printing

How to use the Audio Practice Tests

1. Put your disk into the CD drive of your computer.
2. Click on "My Computer" on your desktop.
3. You will now see "ACV&SS-SCHEG"
4. Click on that disk.
5. When it opens, find the folder "Audio Practice Tests" and click on it.
6. Find the chapter or page number that corresponds to the words that you want to hear and click on that file.
7. The Audio Practice Tests will open in virtually any audio program that is installed on your computer.
8. You may now hear the words pronounced. You may "pause" the word dictation, "reverse" to repeat a word, or "play" as many times as you'd like.
9. The Audio Practice Tests may be used as a pretest, to learn the proper pronunciation of the words, or you may test yourself on their proper spelling. Simply write the words on a sheet of paper as they are dictated and then turn to the proper page (as directed at the end of each test) to correct your answers.
10. If your school subscribes to WebCt or Blackboard, you may be able to listen to the audio clips and type the words into the practice tests online in one of those programs.

How to use the Interactive Puzzles

1. Click on the <u>blue Internet Explorer e files</u> relating to the chapter puzzle that you want to do. The puzzle should now appear and be ready for your use. If the puzzles do not open, look on the screen for a message that says to download Java. Proceed to the next page and follow the instructions on how to do that. If you install Java and the puzzles do not open, follow the rest of the directions for setting up your computer to use the Interactive Puzzles (this should only be necessary for older machines). The contents of the "Interactive Puzzles" folder may also be copied to a folder on your C drive. Simply create a new folder, label it "interactive Puzzles," and drag and drop **ALL** of the **<u>puzzle files</u>** into that folder.

If you Receive a Message to Install Java

1. If your computer does not have "Java" installed, you will have to go to WWW.Java.Com and download a free copy of Java to install on your computer.

2. You will then be ready to use the interactive puzzles on the disk. Open your *Advancing College Vocabulary & Spelling Skills* CD and find the folder labeled "Interactive Puzzles."

3. Click on the blue Internet Explorer **e** files relating to the chapter puzzle that you want to do. The puzzle should now appear and be ready for your use. The contents of the "Interactive Puzzles" folder may also be copied to a folder on your C drive. Simply create a new folder, label it "interactive Puzzles," and (as above) drag and drop **ALL** of the **puzzle files** into that folder.

Further Directions for Setting up the Interactive Puzzles
(Usually not needed except in the case of older machines running older operating systems)

4. Open your C drive and find the folder labeled "Programs".

5. Open the "Programs" folder.

6. Find the folder labeled "Internet Explorer" and open it.

7. Make the window' box smaller by dragging the sides to form a smaller view.

8. Now locate the drive containing your *Advancing College Vocabulary & Spelling Skills* CD and find the folder labeled "Puzzle Software."

9. Open that folder, create a smaller window and place it next to the "Internet Explorer" window.

10. Choose "Select all" from the edit menu for the "Puzzle Software", and then drag all of the highlighted files over into the "Internet Explorer" folder. Close all windows.

Installing the PowerPoint Reader

1. To install the PowerPoint Reader, simply open the PowerPoint Reader folder and click on the install icon. Follow the directions.

Using the PowerPoint Games

1. After installing the PowerPoint Reader, simply open the folder containing the PowerPoint games and click on the game that you want to play.
2. The games are arranged with the current chapter words making up columns 1-3. Column 4 is comprised of review words (except for chapter 1).
3. When you click on the square, you will be given a word. Write or think of the definition for each word and then check your answers.
4. The game does not automatically keep the score. You will have to do that manually if so desired.

Loading the Adobe Reader

1. After loading the Adobe Reader, you will be able to view, or listen to, the entire workbook on your computer. The font size may be enlarged for easier viewing. Listening to the text being read is often a great help for many students.
2. To load the Adobe Reader, simply open the folder labeled Adobe Reader. Click on the icon and follow the directions that appear on the screen.

Acknowledgements:

Photography Courtesy of:

Cover: Copyright © Nathan and Danielle Scheg

Chapter 1: Copyright © Lawrence Scheg

Chapter 2: Copyright © Lawrence Scheg

Chapter 3: Copyright © Leslieann C. Scheg

Chapter 4: Copyright © Lawrence Scheg

Chapter 5: Copyright © Nathan and Danielle Scheg

Chapter 6: Copyright © Nathan and Danielle Scheg

Chapter 7: Copyright © Nathan and Danielle Scheg

Chapter 8: Courtesy of   U S Fish and Wildlife Service

Chapter 9: Courtesy of U S National Oceanic and Atmospheric Administration

Chapter 10: Courtesy of U S National Oceanic and Atmospheric Administration

Chapter 11: Courtesy of U S National Oceanic and Atmospheric Administration

Chapter 12: Courtesy of U S National Oceanic and Atmospheric Administration

Chapter 13: Courtesy of U S National Oceanic and Atmospheric Administration

Chapter 14: Courtesy of U S National Oceanic and Atmospheric Administration

Chapter 15: Courtesy of NASA

Chapter 16: Courtesy of NASA

Chapter 17: Courtesy of U S National Oceanic and Atmospheric Administration

Chapter 18: Courtesy of U S National Oceanic and Atmospheric Administration

Chapter 19: Copyright © Lawrence Scheg

Chapter 20: Copyright © Lawrence Scheg

Chapter 21: Copyright © Lawrence Scheg

Chapter 22: Copyright © Lawrence Scheg

Chapter 23: Copyright © Lawrence Scheg

Chapter 24: Copyright © Lawrence Scheg

Contents

Plus … This edition contains a CD Rom that includes: The entire Vocabulary book in e-book format, ReadPlease © software, interactive puzzles, audio practice tests, and printable study cards containing the vocabulary word and letter grouped vocabulary word on one side and the definition on the reverse.

Advancing College Vocabulary & Spelling Skills

Altercation
Debilitate
Insidious
Appendix
Dispersed
Ludicrous
Catalyst
Effigy
Migraine
Conspiracy
Fluoride

Naive
Contaminant
Implemented
Paranoid

I.) Use context to arrive at meaning. Complete the following sentences with words that are familiar to you and that make sense in each sentence. You may write more than one word choice for each blank space. <u>Do not</u> look at or study the new words yet. Answers will vary and your instructor will discuss them with you.

1. There was a(n) _____ at the local bar last night after several patrons had too much to drink.
2. Sudden illnesses can often _____ a previously healthy person.
3. The _____ explanations clearly showed the trickery behind their actions.
4. No one really seems to know why the _____ exists at the base of the large intestine.
5. Pamphlets were _____ over the city from helicopters and airplanes.
6. Some of the ridiculous explanations seemed _____ even to those who knew little about toxic waste.
7. One concerned citizen served as a _____ to get other citizens involved.
8. The protesters burned a(n) _____ of the Governor.
9. Household cleaners can cause severe _____ headaches in some people.
10. Sometimes we must ask ourselves, "Is it a _____ or are people perhaps just ignorant of many of the hazards that exist.
11. On the toothpaste box, it warns us that a child using more than a pea sized amount of _____toothpaste in brushing their teeth should be referred to the Poison Control Agency or the local Emergency room.
12. It does not benefit you to be _____ about life's dangers.
13. Do you ever wonder what _____ might be buried in your neighborhood?
14. After Love Canal, many new laws were _____ but we still have toxic chemicals in our environment.
15. Am I _____, or is everyone really looking at me?

II.) ***Study the words and definitions below.*** These words and definitions are also on the enclosed CD Rom and may be printed out as study cards. The words are broken into letter groupings for easier spelling. Also, that is followed by a common definition, and common forms of the word that you might encounter. Your instructor will pronounce the words for you or you may want to use an audio dictionary for more help.

1. **altercation** (al/ter/ca/tion) heated argument, quarrel, disagreement, contention, hostility.
2. **appendix** (app/en/dix) supplementary, often considered useless, attachment of the large intestine.
3. **catalyst** (ca/tal/yst) stimulus, incitement, energizer, activator.
4. **conspiracy** (con/spir/acy) an agreement to do a wrong or subversive act, intrigue, sedition, scheme, plot. Also: **conspirator, conspiracies.**
5. **contaminant** (con/tam/i/nant) pollutant, poison. Also: **contamination.**
6. **debilitate** (de/bil/i/tate) drain of energy, fatigue, weaken, exhaust. Also: **debilitation, debilitates, debilitated, debilitating.**
7. **dispersed** (dis/per/sed) scattered, broke up, disbanded, sprinkled. Also: **disperse, dispersing, dispersal, disperses, dispersion.**
8. **effigy** (eff/i/gy) a figure or stuffed dummy representing a hated person, likeness of a hated person.
9. **fluoride** (fl/uor/ide) binding of fluorine with another chemical. (See fluorine for more details) highly corrosive and poisonous chemical as pure fluorine (used in atomic bomb making, added to toothpaste(see warning on box), added to drinking water in many areas).
10. **implemented** (im/ple/men/ted) brought into use, caused to begin. Also: **implement, implementation, implementing, implements.**
11. **insidious** (in/sid/ious) treacherous, devious, deceitful, tricky, underhanded, manipulative. Also: **insidiously, insidiousness.**
12. **ludicrous** (lu/di/cr/ous) ridiculous, laughable, silly, absurd, outlandish, nutty.
13. **migraine** (mi/gr/ain/e) severe headache often including nausea, sharp almost unbearable pain, sometimes vomiting and/or visual pain and/or visual disturbance.
14. **naıve**(naı/ve) childlike, unsophisticated, innocent, uncritical.
15. **paranoid** (par/a/noid) exhibiting extreme fear, mental instability, neurotic.

III.) ***Match the words with their definitions.*** Draw a line connecting each word with its correct definition.

1.	altercation	a. treacherous
2.	appendix	b. heated argument
3.	catalyst	c. poisonous chemical
4.	conspiracy	d. stuffed dummy used as symbol
5.	contaminant	e. ridiculous
6.	debilitate	f. caused to begin
7.	dispersed	g. severe headache
8.	effigy	h. scattered
9.	fluoride	i. pollutant
10.	implemented	j. drain of energy
11.	insidious	k. supplementary
12.	ludicrous	l. subversive act
13.	migraine	m. activator
14.	naïve	n. exhibiting extreme fear
15.	paranoid	o. uncritical

IV.) ***Puzzle work.*** Now try the interactive puzzle. Put the CD (that came with your workbook) into the computer, and work the puzzle. A paper copy of the puzzle is also included at the end of this chapter.

V.)   **Write the correct new word in each sentence below:**

appendix	conspiracy	altercation	contaminant	catalyst
insidious	migraine	naïve	paranoid	ludicrous
debilitate	effigy	dispersed	implemented	fluoride

1. There was a(n) ___altercation___ at the local bar last night after several patrons had too much to drink.
2. Sudden illnesses can often ___debilitate___ a previously healthy person..
3. The ___insidious___ explanations clearly showed the trickery behind their actions.
4. No one really seems to know why the ___appendix___ exists at the base of the large intestine.
5. Pamphlets were ___dispersed___ over the city from helicopters and airplanes.
6. Some of the ridiculous explanations seemed ___ludicrous___ even to those who knew little about toxic waste.
7. One concerned citizen served as a ___catalyst___ to get other citizens involved.
8. The protesters burned a(n) ___Effigy___ of the Governor.
9. Household cleaners can cause severe ___Migraine___ headaches in some people.
10. Sometimes we must ask ourselves, "Is it a ___Conspiracy___ or are people perhaps just ignorant of many of the hazards that exist.
11. On the toothpaste box, it warns us that a child using more than a pea sized amount of ___fluoride___ toothpaste in brushing their teeth should be referred to the Poison Control Agency or the local Emergency room.
12. It does not benefit you to be ___naïve___ about life's dangers.
13. Do you ever wonder what ___contaminant___ might be buried in your neighborhood?
14. After Love Canal, many new laws were ___implemented___ but we still have toxic chemicals in our environment.
15. Am I ___paranoid___, or is everyone really looking at me?

VI.) Are you ready to take the practice test? You may take the practice test as many times as you want to.   Simply insert the CD that came with book into your computer, go to "My Computer", open the CD by clicking on it, find the Practice test folder, choose this chapter's practice test and begin. (You will need a sheet of paper to write your answers on.) When finished, turn back to this chapter and correct your test. The answers are in the same order as exercise II.

VII.) Write a sentence for each new word. Are you ready to use the new words? Write a sentence for each new word.

appendix	conspiracy	altercation	contaminant	catalyst
insidious	migraine	naïve	paranoid	ludicrous
debilitate	effigy	dispersed	implemented	fluoride

1. _____
2. _____
3. _____
4. _____
5. _____
6. _____
7. _____
8. _____
9. _____
10. _____
11. _____
12. _____
13. _____
14. _____
15. _____

VIII.) Your instructor may ask you to do the puzzle on the next page. It is the same as the one on your CD. You are able to do it here once or on the CD as many times as you'd like.

Across

1. Scattered, broke up, disbanded, sprinkled.

3. Severe headache often including nausea, sharp almost unbearable pain, sometimes vomiting and/or visual and/or visual disturbance.

6. An agreement to do wrong or subversive act, intrigue, sedition, scheme, plot.

7. Childlike, unsophisticated, innocent, uncritical.

10. Binding of fluorine with another chemical.

11. A figure or stuffed dummy representing a hated person, likeness of a hated person.

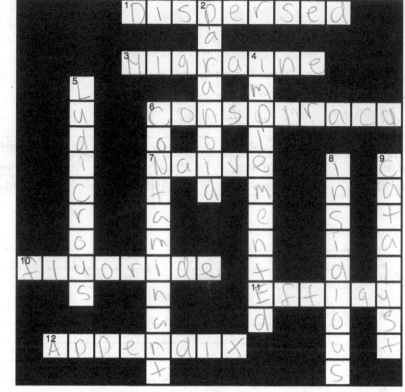

12. Supplementary, often considered useless, attachment of the large intestine

Down

2. Exhibiting extreme fear, mental instability, neurotic.

4. Brought into use, caused to begin.

5. Ridiculous, laughable, silly, absurd, outlandish, nutty.

6. Pollutant, poison.

8. Treacherous, devious, deceitful, tricky, underhanded, manipulative.

9. Stimulus, incitement, energized, activator.

Rewrite your words/Practice Test

New word: **Practice writing the new word:**

Rewrite your words/Practice test

New word: **Practice writing the new word:**

Advancing College Vocabulary & Spelling Skills

I.) Use context to arrive at meaning. Complete the following sentences with words that are familiar to you and that make sense in each sentence. You may write more than one word choice for each blank space. <u>Do not</u> look at or study the new words yet. Answers will vary and your instructor will discuss them with you.

Aggravation
Epidermialugist
Periphery
Alliance
Exacerbated
Preliminary
Bureaucracy
Exuberance
Stealthy
Demarcation
Imminent
Subsequently
Disfiguration
Memorandum
Superficial

1. Brandon was feeling a lot of ___frustration___ because of the constant interruptions of his co-workers.
2. The ___Doctor___ was trying to find the cause of the Monkey Pox.
3. No one could go beyond the ___Outskirts___ of the town because of the quarantine.
4. The United States formed a(n) ___alliance___ with Great Britain over the problems of the Middle East.
5. Putting heat lotion on the sunburn ___relieves___ the pain.
6. According to the ___police___ report no weapons of mass destruction were found, but later searches turned up several sites.
7. Even a good government can be bogged down by its ___citizens___.
8. The initial ___intentions___ of the new recruits was soon lost as they realized the difficult tasks that lie ahead.
9. The Stealth Bomber can move in on its enemies in a very ___discreet___ manner.
10. The line of ___separation___ was set and the enemy forces were told not to cross it.
11. Many were looking for his ___Imminent___ return but it did not occur as soon as they expected.
12. Because he did not arrive when they were expecting him, many were ___greatly___ disappointed.
13. The ___injury___ that Tony suffered, when the battery blew up, would unfortunately stay with him the rest of his life.
14. In her ___speech___, the Senator put forth her views on the issues at hand.
15. Officer Schultz suffered only a(n) ___Superficial___ wound during the gun battle with the deranged criminal.

II.) *Study the words and definitions below.* These words and definitions are also on the enclosed CD Rom and may be printed out as study cards. The words are broken into letter groupings for easier spelling. Also, that is followed by a common definition, and common forms of the word that you might encounter. Your instructor will pronounce the words for you or you may want to use an audio dictionary for more help.

1. **aggravation** (agg/ra/va/tion) annoyance, irritation, harassment, vexation. Also: **aggravate,**.
2. **alliance** (all/ia/nce) friendly association, coalition, affiliation.
3. **bureaucracy** (bur/eau/cr/acy) governmental administration mainly through bureaus, branches or departments; inflexible rules and red tape. Also: **bureau, bureaucratic, bureaucrat.**
4. **demarcation** (de/mar/ca/tion) setting of boundaries, marking off, setting limits, distinguishing, separation.
5. **disfiguration** (dis/fig/ur/a/tion) to damage or mar something or someone, deform, distort, misshape. Also: **disfigure, disfigurement.**
6. **epidemiologist** (ep/i/dem/iol/o/gist) study of disease and its causes, spread, and control. Also: **epidemiology.**
7. **exacerbated** (ex/a/cer/ba/ted) increased in severity, magnified, amplified, escalated, intensified. Also: **exacerbate, exacerbating, exacerbates, exacerbation.**
8. **exuberance** (ex/u/ber/ance) feeling of intense joy, elation, jubilation, exhilaration. Also: **exuberant.**
9. **imminent** (imm/i/nent) soon to occur, impending.
10. **memorandum** (mem/or/an/dum) a written communication, bulletin, note, correspondence, reminder. Also: **memorandums or memoranda.**
11. **periphery** (per/i/ph/ery) perimeter, boundary line, border line.
12. **preliminary** (pre/lim/in/ary) initial, introductory, preparatory.
13. **stealthy** (st/eal/thy) secret, hidden, deceptive, secret. Also: **stealthily.**
14. **subsequently** (sub/se/quent/ly) following after in time order, next, successive. Also: **subsequent.**
15. **superficial** (su/per/fi/cial) shallow, near the surface, insignificant. Also: **superficially, superficiality.**

III.) *Match the words with their definitions.* Draw a line connecting each word with its correct definition.

1. aggravation
2. alliance
3. bureaucracy
4. demarcation
5. disfiguration
6. epidemiologist
7. exacerbated
8. exuberance
9. imminent
10. memorandum
11. periphery
12. preliminary
13. stealthy
14. subsequently
15. superficial

a. border-line
b. insignificant
c. following after in time
d. elation, joy
e. secret, hidden
f. setting of boundaries
g. soon to occur
h. written communication
i. magnified
j. one who studies disease
k. friendly association
l. annoyance
m. deformation
n. inflexible rules
o. introductory

IV.) *Puzzle work.* Now try the interactive puzzle. Put the CD (that came with your workbook) into the computer, and work the puzzle. A paper copy of the puzzle is also included at the end of this chapter.

V.)   Write the correct new word in each sentence below:

epidemiologist	exuberance	memorandum	exacerbated	imminent
aggravation	bureaucracy	disfiguration	demarcation	alliance
preliminary	subsequently	periphery	stealthy	superficial

1. Brandon was feeling a lot of _aggravation_ because of the constant interruptions of his co-workers.
2. The _epidemiologist_ was trying to find the cause of the Monkey Pox.
3. No one could go beyond the _periphery_ of the town because of the quarantine.
4. The United States formed a(n) _alliance_ with Great Britain over the problems of the Middle East.
5. Putting heat lotion on the sunburn _exacerbated_ the pain.
6. According to the _preliminary_ report no weapons of mass destruction were found, but later searches turned up several sites.
7. Even a good government can be bogged down by its _bureaucracy_.
8. The initial _exuberance_ of the new recruits was soon lost as they realized the difficult tasks that lie ahead.
9. The Stealth Bomber can move in on its enemies in a very _stealthy_ manner.
10. The line of _demarcation_ was set and the enemy forces were told not to cross it.
11. Many were looking for his _imminent_ return but it did not occur as soon as they expected.
12. Because he did not arrive when they were expecting him, many were _subsequently_ disappointed.
13. The _disfiguration_ that Tony suffered, when the battery blew up, would unfortunately stay with him the rest of his life.
14. In her _memorandum_, the Senator put forth her views on the issues at hand.
15. Officer Schultz suffered only a(n) _superficial_ wound during the gun battle with the deranged criminal.

VI.) Are you ready to take the practice test? You may take the practice test as many times as you want to. Simply insert the CD that came with book into your computer, go to "My Computer", open the CD by clicking on it, find the Practice test folder, choose this chapter's practice test and begin. (You will need a sheet of paper to write your answers on.) When finished, turn back to this chapter and correct your test. The answers are in the same order as exercise II.

VII.) Write a sentence for each new word. Are you ready to use the new words? Write a sentence for each new word.

epidemiologist	exuberance	memorandum	exacerbated	imminent
aggravation	bureaucracy	disfiguration	demarcation	alliance
preliminary	subsequently	periphery	stealthy	superficial

1. _____
2. _____
3. _____
4. _____
5. _____
6. _____
7. _____
8. _____
9. _____
10. _____
11. _____
12. _____
13. _____
14. _____
15. _____

VIII.) Your instructor may ask you to do the puzzle on the next page. It is the same as the one on your CD. You are able to do it here once or on the CD as many times as you'd like.

Across

2. Perimeter, boundary line, border line.

4. A written communication, bulletin, note, correspondence, reminder.

6. Feeling of intense joy, elation, jubilation, exhilaration.

8. Friendly association, coalition, affiliation.

9. Following after in time order, next, successive.

10. Secret, hidden, deceptive.

Down

1. Study of disease and its causes, spread, and control.

3. Increased in severity, magnified, amplified, escalated, intensified.

5. Setting of boundaries, marking off, setting limits, distinguishing, separation.

7. Governmental administration mainly through bureaus, branches or departments; inflexible rules and red tape.

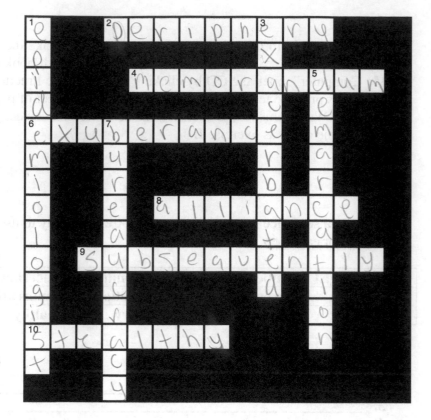

Rewrite your words/Practice Test

New word:		Practice writing the new word:	

Rewrite your words/Practice test

New word: **Practice writing the new word:**

Advancing College Vocabulary & Spelling Skills

I.)   Use context to arrive at meaning. Complete the following sentences with words that are familiar to you and that make sense in each sentence. You may write more than one word choice for each blank space. <u>Do not</u> look at or study the new words yet. Answers will vary and your instructor will discuss them with you.

aesthetics
exemplary
profusion
apprehension
hypochondriac
reluctant
circumventing
indoctrinate
repercussion
concoction
inexplicably

1. People often purchase an automobile more based on __appearance__ than functionality.
2. Josie received an award for her __magnificent__ service to the wilderness project.
3. There was a(n) __herd__ of frogs this year at the pond near our house.
4. Stewart felt a lot of __excitement__ as he sat waiting for his interview to begin.
5. It's sad that some doctors label people as __disabled__ just because they can't find a solution to their problems.
6. Kim was __eager__ to try the strange looking food that Jesse had cooked for her.
7. Jim tried __hacking__ the system and ended up in legal difficulties.
8. Many cults seek new members that they can __recruit__ and then control.
9. There will be a serious __consequences__ if you don't pay your taxes correctly.
10. Lisa made a strange looking __smoothie__ for Katie and called it her green energy health drink.
11. All members of the committee were __shockingly__ silent when the chairperson suddenly resigned.
12. Too many clothes and too much heat can make a(n) __spontaneous__ Combustion fire in a dryer.

epileptic
perpendicular
treacherous

13. Exposure to some pesticides may trigger a(n) __strong__ seizure.
14. Rose Avenue is __close__ to Tulip Drive, which intersects with it at the north corner.
15. Going over Niagara Falls in a wooden barrel is a very __courageous__ thing to do but a few have tried it.

II.) *Study the words and definitions below.* These words and definitions are also on the enclosed CD Rom and may be printed out as study cards. The words are broken into letter groupings for easier spelling. Also, that is followed by a common definition, and common forms of the word that you might encounter. Your instructor will pronounce the words for you or you may want to use an audio dictionary for more help.

1. **aesthetics or (esthetics)** (aes/the/tics) conception of what is beautiful.
2. **apprehension** (app/re/hen/sion) fearful, uneasy, worrisome, anxiety, fretfulness. Also: **apprehensive.**
3. **circumventing** (cir/cum/vent/ing) avoiding, getting around something without going through the proper channels.
4. **concoction** (con/coc/tion) mixture.
5. **epileptic** (ep/i/lep/tic) motor, psychological, or sensory malfunctioning that may lead to convulsive seizures.
6. **exemplary** (ex/em/plary) praiseworthy, notable, meritorious, admirable.
7. **hypochondriac** (hy/po/chon/driac) one who imagines having illnesses when they do not exist.
8. **indoctrinate** (in/doc/trin/ate) to instruct into a certain doctrine.
9. **inexplicably** (in/ex/pli/ca/bly) difficult to explain, ambiguous. Also: **inexplicable.**
10. **perpendicular** (per/pen/di/cu/lar) vertical, erect, upright.
11. **profusion** (pro/fu/sion) abundant supply, plentiful, richness, abundance.
12. **reluctant** (re/luc/tant) unwilling, hesitant, resistant, averse.
13. **repercussion** (re/per/cuss/ion) reaction, rebound, recoil, reciprocal motion.
14. **spontaneous** (spon/tan/eous) self-generated; instantaneous, immediate.
15. **treacherous** (trea/cher/ous) devious, dangerous, manipulative, deceitful, faithless. Also: **treachery, treacherously.**

III.) *Match the words with their definitions.* Draw a line connecting each word with its correct definition.

1. aesthetics	a. unwilling
2. apprehension	b. instruct into a certain doctrine
3. circumventing	c. vertical
4. concoction	d. abundant supply
5. epileptic	e. malfunctioning & convulsions
6. exemplary	f. dangerous
7. hypochondriac	g. praiseworthy
8. indoctrinate	h. reaction
9. inexplicably	i. imagines illness
10. perpendicular	j. difficult to explain
11. profusion	k. conception of beauty
12. reluctant	l. avoiding
13. repercussion	m. mixture
14. spontaneous	n. self-generated
15. treacherous	o. anxiety

IV.) *Puzzle work.* Now try the interactive puzzle. Put the CD (that came with your workbook) into the computer, and work the puzzle. A paper copy of the puzzle is also included at the end of this chapter.

V.)   Write the correct new word in each sentence below:

circumventing	repercussion	concoction	spontaneous	epileptic
treacherous	aesthetics	profusion	apprehension	reluctant
exemplary	indoctrinate	perpendicular	inexplicably	hypochondriac

1. People often purchase an automobile more based on _aesthetics_ than functionality.
2. Josie received an award for her _exemplary_ service to the wilderness project.
3. There was a(n) _profusion_ of frogs this year at the pond near our house.
4. Stewart felt a lot of _apprehension_ as he sat waiting for his interview to begin.
5. It's sad that some doctors label people as _hypochondriac_ just because they can't find a solution to their problems.
6. Kim was _reluctant_ to try the strange looking food that Jesse had cooked for her.
7. Jim tried _circumventing_ the system and ended up in legal difficulties.
8. Many cults seek new members that they can _indoctrinate_ and then control.
9. There will be a serious _repercussion_ if you don't pay your taxes correctly.
10. Lisa made a strange looking _concoction_ for Katie and called it her green energy health drink.
11. All members of the committee were _inexplicably_ silent when the chairperson suddenly resigned.
12. Too many clothes and too much heat can make a(n) _spontaneous_ Combustion fire in a dryer.
13. Exposure to some pesticides may trigger a(n) _epileptic_ seizure.
14. Rose avenue is _perpendicular_ to Tulip drive which intersects with it at the north corner.
15. Going over Niagara Falls in a wooden barrel is a very _treacherous_ thing to do but a few have tried it.

VI.) Are you ready to take the practice test? You may take the practice test as many times as you want to. Simply insert the CD that came with book into your computer, go to "My Computer", open the CD by clicking on it, find the Practice test folder, choose this chapter's practice test and begin. (You will need a sheet of paper to write your answers on.) When finished, turn back to this chapter and correct your test. The answers are in the same order as exercise II.

VII.) Write a sentence for each new word. Are you ready to use the new words? Write a sentence for each new word.

circumventing	repercussion	concoction	spontaneous	epileptic
treacherous	aesthetics	profusion	apprehension	reluctant
exemplary	indoctrinate	perpendicular	inexplicably	hypochondriac

1. _____
2. _____
3. _____
4. _____
5. _____
6. _____
7. _____
8. _____
9. _____
10. _____
11. _____
12. _____
13. _____
14. _____
15. _____

VIII.) Your instructor may ask you to do the puzzle on the next page. It is the same as the one on your CD. You are able to do it here once or on the CD as many times as you'd like.

Across

1. Reaction, rebound, recoil, reciprocal motion

8. Unwilling, hesitant, resistant, averse.

9. Mixture

10. Conception of what is beautiful.

11. Devious, dangerous, manipulative, deceitful, faithless.

Down

2. Motor, psychological, or sensory malfunctioning that may lead to convulsive seizures.

3. Avoiding, getting around something without going through the proper channels.

4. Self-generated; instantaneous, immediate.

5. To instruct into a certain doctrine.

6. One who imagines having illnesses when they do not exist.

7. Fearful, uneasy, worrisome, anxiety, fretfulness.

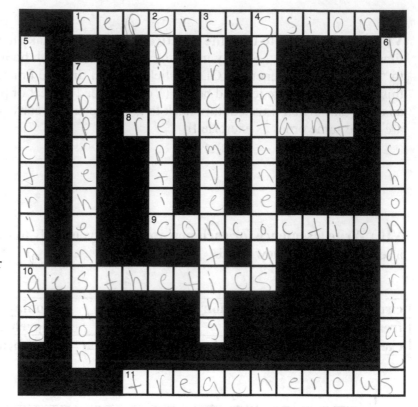

Rewrite your words/Practice Test

New word: **Practice writing the new word:**

Rewrite your words/Practice test

New word:	Practice writing the new word:		

Advancing College Vocabulary & Spelling Skills

I.)   Use context to arrive at meaning. Complete the following sentences with words that are familiar to you and that make sense in each sentence. You may write more than one word choice for each blank space. <u>Do not</u> look at or study the new words yet. Answers will vary and your instructor will discuss them with you.

alchemistic
convulsions
potentiate
barbiturate
dissipated
progenitor

1. The __Chemist__ mixed his potions in an effort to create some bizarre new concoction.
2. After inhaling the chemicals, the chemist went into __Shock__ and later died.
3. Mixing several chemicals together can __increase__ their power.
4. The toxin had a(n) __adverse__ effect causing the victim to lose consciousness.
5. When looking for traces of the original pesticide, it seemed like it had __disposed__ but later it was found that it had changed chemically.
6. Rachel Carson detailed the harmfulness of DDT and later claimed that as a(n) __progenitor__ to later pesticides it seemed relatively mild in order to show us how much more lethal later chemical concoctions became.

Bellicose
extraneous
psychological
constituents
insurgents
supplant
contingency
physiological
vacillate

7. Bees sprayed with some pesticides become very __hostile__ and attacked anyone in sight.
8. Rachel thought the use of pesticides was usually a(n) __ineffective__ exercise since the pest problem usually became worse afterwards.
9. Besides having an effect on the body, many chemicals may also have __psychological__ effects.
10. One of the __constituents__ of most elements is carbon.
11. Most __insurgents__ are hardened soldiers too.
12. The use of pesticides tended to __replace__ more traditional methods of farming.
13. We must be prepared for whatever __crisis__ may arise when insects no longer respond to chemical spraying.
14. One of the __physiological__ results of chemical exposure may be convulsions.
15. Many people __procrastinate__ when it comes to making critical decisions about their long-term health.

II.) **_Study the words and definitions below._** These words and definitions are also on the enclosed CD Rom and may be printed out as study cards. The words are broken into letter groupings for easier spelling. Also, that is followed by a common definition, and common forms of the word that you might encounter. Your instructor will pronounce the words for you or you may want to use an audio dictionary for more help.

1. **alchemistic** (al/chem./is/tic) seemingly magical power of transformation. Also: **alchemy, alchemist, alchemize, alchemistic.**
2. **barbiturate** (bar/bi/tur/ate) a barbituric acid derivatives that acts as a central nervous system depressant; sedative, hypnotic.
3. **bellicose** (bell/i/cose) warlike, agitated, belligerent, combative. Also: **bellicosely, bellicoseness, bellicosity.**
4. **constituents** (con/sti/tu/ents) components, ingredients, part of something else.
5. **contingency** (con/tin/gen/cy) a possibility, an event that may occur, likelihood, eventuality. Also: **contingencies.**
6. **convulsions** (con/vul/sions) seizure, violent turmoil, involuntary muscle contractions, spasm.
7. **dissipated** (diss/i/pa/ted) dispersed, scattered, evaporated; loss of energy. Also: **dissipate, dissipates, dissipating.**
8. **extraneous** (ex/tran/e/ous) nonessential, unnecessary, dispensable, unrelated. Also: **extraneously, extraneousness.**
9. **insurgents** (in/sur/gents) rebels, anarchists, extremists, revolutionaries, terrorists, radicals, insurrectionists.
10. **physiological** (phys/io/log/i/cal) relating to the physical body or its functioning.
11. **potentiate** (po/ten/tia/te) to increase the power of a drug, make more potent. Also: **potentiation.**
12. **progenitor** (pro/gen/i/tor) direct ancestor; founder, originator, creator, inventor.
13. **psychological** (psy/cho/log/i/cal) relating to the mind and its functioning. Also: **psychiatrist, psychology.**
14. **supplant** (supp/lant) to displace, to substitute, usurp, unseat.
15. **vacillate** (vac/ill/ate) oscillate, swing from side to side, falter, hesitate, waver.

III.) *Match the words with their definitions.* Draw a line connecting each word with its correct definition.

1.	alchemist	a. anarchists
2.	barbiturate	b. seizures
3.	bellicose	c. scattered
4.	constituents	d. hesitate
5.	contingency	e. relating to the body
6.	convulsions	f. relating to the mind
7.	dissipated	g. increase the power of
8.	extraneous	h. unseat
9.	insurgents	i. warlike
10.	physiological	j. system depressant
11.	potentiate	k. part of something else
12.	progenitor	l. founder
13.	psychological	m. eventuality
14.	supplant	n. nonessential
15.	vacillate	o. seemingly magical transforming power

IV.) *Puzzle work.* Now try the interactive puzzle. Put the CD (that came with your workbook) into the computer, and work the puzzle. A paper copy of the puzzle is also included at the end of this chapter.

V.)   Write the correct new word in each sentence below:

convulsions	barbiturate	extraneous	constituents	physiological
vacillate	supplant	alchemist	contingency	progenitor
psychological	potentiate	insurgents	bellicose	dissipated

1. The ___alchemist___ mixed his potions in an effort to create some bizarre new concoction.
2. After inhaling the chemicals, the chemist went into ___convulsions___ and later died.
3. Mixing several chemicals together can ___potentiate___ their power.
4. The toxin had a(n) ___barbiturate___ effect causing the victim to lose consciousness.
5. When looking for traces of the original pesticide, it seemed like it had ___dissipated___ but later it was found that it had changed chemically.
6. George Herbert Walker Bush is the ___progenitor___ of George W. Bush.
7. Bees sprayed with some pesticides become very ___bellicose___ and attacked anyone in sight.
8. Rachel thought the use of pesticides was usually a(n) ___extraneous___ exercise since the pest problem usually became worse afterwards.
9. Besides having an effect on the body, many chemicals may also have ___psychological___ effects.
10. One of the ___constituents___ of many molecules is carbon.
11. The United States troops faced many ___insurgents___ in Iraq.
12. The use of pesticides tended to ___supplant___ more traditional methods of farming.
13. We must be prepared for whatever ___contingency___ may arise when insects no longer respond to chemical spraying.
14. One of the ___physiological___ results of chemical exposure may be convulsions.
15. Many people ___vacillate___ when it comes to making critical decisions about their long-term health.

VI.) Are you ready to take the practice test? You may take the practice test as many times as you want to.   Simply insert the CD that came with book into your computer, go to "My Computer", open the CD by clicking on it, find the Practice test folder, choose this chapter's practice test and begin. (You will need a sheet of paper to write your answers on.) When finished, turn back to this chapter and correct your test. The answers are in the same order as exercise II.

VII.) Write a sentence for each new word. Are you ready to use the new words? Write a sentence for each new word.

convulsions	barbiturate	extraneous	constituents	physiological
vacillate	supplant	alchemist	contingency	progenitor
psychological	potentiate	insurgents	bellicose	dissipated

1. _____
2. _____
3. _____
4. _____
5. _____
6. _____
7. _____
8. _____
9. _____
10. _____
11. _____
12. _____
13. _____
14. _____
15. _____

VIII.) Your instructor may ask you to do the puzzle on the next page. It is the same as the one on your CD. You are able to do it here once or on the CD as many times as you'd like.

Across

4. To increase the power of a drug, make more potent.

7. A possibility, an event that may occur, likelihood, eventuality

8. Nonessential, unnecessary, dispensable, unrelated.

9. Dispersed, scattered, evaporated; loss of energy.

10. Relating to the mind and its functioning.

Down

1. To displace, to substitute, usurp, unseat.

2. A barbituric acid derivatives that acts as a central nervous system depressant; sedative, hypnotic.

3. Warlike, agitated, belligerent, combative.

5. Seizure, violent turmoil, involuntary muscle contractions, spasm.

6. Seemingly magical power of transformation.

Rewrite your words/Practice Test

New word:		Practice writing the new word:	

Rewrite your words/Practice test

New word: **Practice writing the new word:**

Advancing College Vocabulary & Spelling Skills

I.) Use context to arrive at meaning. Complete the following sentences with words that are familiar to you and that make sense in each sentence. You may write more than one word choice for each blank space. <u>Do not</u> look at or study the new words yet. Answers will vary and your instructor will discuss them with you.

anesthetic
enzyme
pandemic
carcinogen
epidemic
pharma-
cologist
configuration

manipulation
suburbanite
degenerative
necrosis
therapeutic
disparity
oxidation
trepidation

1. As the _antibiotics_ wore off, Donald began to feel the pain of the surgery.
2. Every _organ_ is important to the proper functioning of the cells in our body.
3. In the 1920's, the flu became _fatal_ and people were dying all over the world.
4. It's not always possible to identify every _sickness_ but cancer is nevertheless on the rise.
5. A small village suffered a(n) _plague_ of Ebola virus that killed nearly everyone in the village.
6. The _doctor_ did not know which medicine would fight the disease.
7. The biologist had never seen such a(n) _abundance_ of chemicals before.
8. Just by the _cluster_ of a few genes, Dr. Death was able to create a new disease.
9. Virtually every _citizen_ needs to mow the lawn once a week.
10. Our society suffers from many _vital_ diseases whose causes are often unknown.
11. Scientists know that certain pesticides often bring about _killing_ of liver cells which may lead to death.
12. The need for _prescribed_ medicine would not be so great if our environment wasn't so polluted.
13. There is often a(n) _line_ between the safety claimed for a product and its actual safety record.
14. The body receives much of its energy from a process called _homostasis_.
15. It would be with much _concern_ that I would use pesticides in my environment.

II.)   *Study the words and definitions below.* These words and definitions are also on the enclosed CD Rom and may be printed out as study cards. The words are broken into letter groupings for easier spelling. Also, that is followed by a common definition, and common forms of the word that you might encounter. Your instructor will pronounce the words for you or you may want to use an audio dictionary for more help.

1. **anesthetic** (an/es/the/tic) a numbing agent, sedative. Also: **anesthesia, anesthetically.**
2. **carcinogen** (car/cin/o/gen) something that causes cancer. Also: **carcinogenic, carcinogenicity.**
3. **configuration** (con/fig/ur/a/tion) arrangement of items, structure, form, shape, physical makeup, construction, composition.
4. **degenerative** (de/gen/er/a/tive) breaking down, moving away from a healthy state, regressive.
5. **disparity** (dis/par/ity) incompatibility, unequality, disagreeableness, dissimilarity, inconsistency. Also: **disparities.**
6. **enzyme** (en/zy/me) one of many proteins that serve as biochemical catalysts.
7. **epidemic** (ep/i/dem/ic) a disease that is widespread and very contagious, plague, pestilence, epidemic, scourge, pandemic.
8. **manipulation** (man/i/pu/la/tion) the controlling of others by devious means.
9. **necrosis** (ne/cro/sis) death of cells or tissues. Also: **necrotic.**
10. **oxidation** (ox/i/da/tion) combining of a substance with oxygen; a reaction in which the substance loses electrons and will more readily combine with another substance.
11. **pandemic** (pan/dem/ic) widespread, expansive, vast, epidemic.
12. **pharmacologist** (pharm/a/col/o/gist) one who mixes legal drugs and medicines. Also: **pharmacology, pharmacological.**
13. **suburbanite** (su/bur/ban/ite) a person who lives in an area just outside of a city. Also: **suburban, suburb, suburbanize, suburbia.**
14. **therapeutic** (ther/a/peu/tic) possessing healing power, medicinal, restorative, salutary, curative. Also: **therapeutically, therapeutical, therapy.**
15. **trepidation** (tre/pi/da/tion) apprehension, state of alarm, dread, trembling.

III.) *Match the words with their definitions.* Draw a line connecting each word with its correct definition.

1. anesthetic
2. carcinogen
3. configuration
4. degenerative
5. disparity
6. enzyme
7. epidemic
8. manipulation
9. necrosis
10. oxidation
11. pandemic
12. pharmacologist
13. suburbanite
14. therapeutic
15. trepidation

a. apprehension
b. widespread disease
c. living in the suburbs
d. combining with oxygen
e. death of cells or tissues
f. numbing agent
g. biochemical catalyst
h. one who mixes medicines
i. possessing healing power
j. incompatibility
k. breaking down
l. structure
m. cancer causing
n. control of others
o. expansive

IV.) *Puzzle work.* Now try the interactive puzzle. Put the CD (that came with your workbook) into the computer, and work the puzzle. A paper copy of the puzzle is also included at the end of this chapter.

V.)   Write the correct new word in each sentence below:

trepidation	therapeutic	suburbanite	pharmacologist	pandemic
anesthetic	enzyme	epidemic	carcinogen	manipulation
configuration	degenerative	necrosis	oxidation	disparity

1. As the __anesthetic__ wore off, Donald began to feel the pain of the surgery.
2. Every __enzyme__ is important to the proper functioning of the cells in our body.
3. In the 1920's the flu became __pandemic__ and people were dying all over the world.
4. It's not always possible to identify every __carcinogen__ but cancer is nevertheless on the rise.
5. A small village suffered a(n) __epidemic__ of Ebola virus that killed nearly everyone in the village.
6. The __pharmacologist__ did not know which medicine would fight the disease.
7. The biologist had never seen such a(n) __configuration__ of chemicals before.
8. Just by the __manipulation__ of a few genes, Dr. Death was able to create a new disease.
9. Virtually every __suburbanite__ needs to mow the lawn once a week.
10. Our society suffers from many __degenerative__ diseases whose causes are often unknown.
11. Scientists know that certain pesticides often bring about __necrosis__ of liver cells which may lead to death.
12. The need for __therapeutic__ medicine would not be so great if our environment wasn't so polluted.
13. There is often a(n) __disparity__ between the safety claimed for a product and its actual safety record.
14. The body receives much of its energy from a process called __oxidation__.
15. It would be with much __trepidation__ that I would use chemicals in my environment.

VI.) Are you ready to take the practice test? You may take the practice test as many times as you want to. Simply insert the CD that came with book into your computer, go to "My Computer", open the CD by clicking on it, find the Practice test folder, choose this chapter's practice test and begin. (You will need a sheet of paper to write your answers on.) When finished, turn back to this chapter and correct your test. The answers are in the same order as exercise II.

VII.) Write a sentence for each new word. Are you ready to use the new words? Write a sentence for each new word.

trepidation	therapeutic	suburbanite	pharmacologist	pandemic
anesthetic	enzyme	epidemic	carcinogen	manipulation
configuration	degenerative	necrosis	oxidation	disparity

1. _____
2. _____
3. _____
4. _____
5. _____
6. _____
7. _____
8. _____
9. _____
10. _____
11. _____
12. _____
13. _____
14. _____
15. _____

VIII.) Your instructor may ask you to do the puzzle on the next page. It is the same as the one on your CD. You are able to do it here once or on the CD as many times as you'd like.

Across

1. One who mixes legal drugs and medicines.

5. Death of cells or tissues.

7. Breaking down, moving away from a healthy state, regressive.

8. A numbing agent, sedative

9. Combining of a substance with oxygen; a reaction in which the substance loses electrons and will more readily combine with another substance.

10. One of many proteins that serve as biochemical catalysts.

Down

2. Possessing healing power, medicinal, restorative, salutary, curative.

3. The controlling of others by devious means

4. Arrangement of items, structure, form, shape, physical makeup, construction, composition.

6. Apprehension, state of alarm, dread, trembling

7. Incompatibility, unequal, disagreeable, dissimilar, inconsistency.

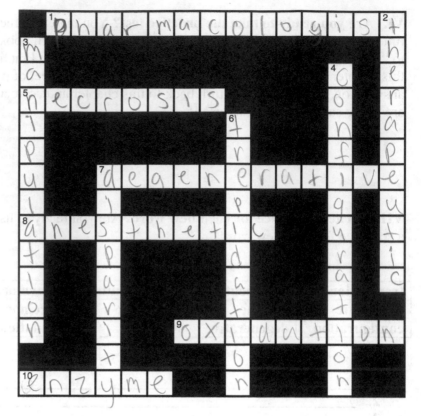

Rewrite your words/Practice Test

New word: **Practice writing the new word:**

Rewrite your words/Practice test

New word:	Practice writing the new word:		

Advancing College Vocabulary & Spelling Skills

I.) Use context to arrive at meaning. Complete the following sentences with words that are familiar to you and that make sense in each sentence. You may write more than one word choice for each blank space. <u>Do not</u> look at or study the new words yet. Answers will vary and your instructor will discuss them with you.

capricious
emanating
metabolism
cascade
entomologist
mutagen
caustic
entrepre-
neur
precarious
defoliant
flamboyant
subsidiary
disseminate
malignant
systemic

1. The Prisoner's _____unexplainable_____ *unpredictable* behavior made everyone nervous because they never knew what he would do next.
2. There was a soft light _____beaming_____ from just over the horizon.
3. Some people's _____metabolism_____ is slower than others which causes them to gain weight more easily.
4. The rapids began to _____flow_____ over the rocks just south of the falls.
5. The _____insplore_____ could not understand why so many insects were dying.
6. Scientists could not determine what _____element_____ had caused the strange mutations.
7. Lye is a very _____toxic_____ substance and it burns the skin very easily.
8. Larry is such a great _____boss_____; he has started several successful businesses.
9. Starting a business on borrowed money can be a very _____responsible_____ undertaking.
10. Agent Orange was used in Vietnam as a _____toxin_____ that stripped leaves from the jungle trees.
11. Her _____beautiful_____ outfit caught the attention of everyone at the party.
12. Lincoln Mercury is a _____branch_____ of the Ford Motor Company.
13. Concerned citizens tried to _____persuade_____ information about the hazards of fluoride in toothpaste and water supplies.
14. Alicia didn't know the cause of the _____hormonal_____ growth and was afraid she would die.
15. Scientists have developed a(n) _____precarious_____ drug that slightly poisons the blood of dogs and cats so fleas that bite them will die almost instantly.

II.)   *Study the words and definitions below.* These words and definitions are also on the enclosed CD Rom and may be printed out as study cards. The words are broken into letter groupings for easier spelling. Also, that is followed by a common definition, and common forms of the word that you might encounter. Your instructor will pronounce the words for you or you may want to use an audio dictionary for more help.

1. **capricious** (ca/pri/cious) impulsive, unpredictable, whimsical, fickle, unpredictable. Also: **capriciously, capriciousness.**
2. **cascade** (cas/cade) waterfall, series of waterfalls over tumbling over rocks. Also: **cascades, cascading, cascaded.**
3. **caustic** (caus/tic) corrosive, able to eat away at metal and other substances, erosive.
4. **defoliant** (de/fol/iant) a chemical used to destroy the leaves on plants.
5. **disseminate** (diss/em/in/ate) spread, scatter, diffuse, strew, distribute. Also: **dissemination, disseminator.**
6. **emanating** (em/an/a/ting) coming from; sending forth, flowing out; originating.
7. **entomologist** (en/to/mol/o/gist) one who study insects. Also: **entomology.**
8. **entrepreneur** (en/tre/pre/neur) a founder of a business venture. Also: **entrepreneurial, entrepreneurialism, entrepreneurship.**
9. **flamboyant** (flam/boy/ant) showy, highly ornate, gaudy, ostentatious, garish.
10. **malignant** (mal/ig/nant) cancerous, capable of causing death, life-threatening, malevolent. Also: **malignancy.**
11. **metabolism** (me/ta/bol/ism) physical and chemical process that converts food to energy and is necessary for life and health.
12. **mutagen (mut/a/gen)** something that induces or increases mutation in an organism. Also: mutagenic.
13. **precarious** (pre/car/ious) dangerous, hazardous, perilous, risky. Also: **precariously.**
14. **subsidiary** (sub/sid/iary) second in importance, franchise, branch, division, unit, auxiliary.
15. **systemic (sys/tem/ic)** affecting the entire body.

III.) *Match the words with their definitions.* Draw a line connecting each word with its correct definition.

1.	capricious	a. affecting the entire body
2.	cascade	b. chemical that destroys leaves
3.	caustic	c. changing food to energy
4.	defoliant	d. one who studies insects
5.	disseminate	e. founder of a business
6.	emanating	f. cancerous
7.	entomologist	g. creates a mutation
8.	entrepreneur	h. franchise, branch
9.	flamboyant	i. showy
10.	malignant	j. flowing out from
11.	metabolism	k. tumbling over
12.	mutagen	l. corrosive
13.	precarious	m. hazardous
14.	subsidiary	n. distribute
15.	systemic	o. whimsical

IV.) *Puzzle work.* Now try the interactive puzzle. Put the CD (that came with your workbook) into the computer, and work the puzzle. A paper copy of the puzzle is also included at the end of this chapter.

V.)   Write the correct new word in each sentence below:

systemic	malignant	entrepreneur	entomologist	capricious
mutagen	caustic	precarious	emanating	flamboyant
defoliant	cascade	disseminate	metabolism	subsidiary

1. The prisoner's ___Capricious___ behavior made everyone nervous because they never knew what he would do next.
2. There was a soft light ___emanating___ from just over the horizon.
3. Some people's ___metabolism___ is slower than others which causes them to gain weight more easily.
4. The rapids began to ___cascade___ over the rocks just south of the falls.
5. The ___entomologist___ could not understand why so many insects were dying.
6. Scientists could not determine what ___mutagen___ had caused the strange mutations.
7. Lye is a very ___caustic___ substance and it burns the skin very easily.
8. Larry is such a great ___entrepreneur___; he has started several successful businesses.
9. Starting a business on borrowed money can be a very ___precarious___ undertaking.
10. Agent Orange was used in Vietnam as a ___defoliant___ that stripped leaves from the jungle trees.
11. Her ___flamboyant___ outfit caught the attention of everyone at the party.
12. Lincoln Mercury is a ___subsidiary___ of the Ford Motor Company.
13. Concerned citizens tried to ___disseminate___ information about the hazards of fluoride in toothpaste and water supplies.
14. Alicia didn't know the cause of the ___malignant___ growth and was afraid she would die.
15. Scientists have developed a(n) ___systemic___ drug that slightly poisons the blood of dogs and cats so fleas that bite them will die almost instantly.

VI.) Are you ready to take the practice test? You may take the practice test as many times as you want to. Simply insert the CD that came with book into your computer, go to "My Computer", open the CD by clicking on it, find the Practice test folder, choose this chapter's practice test and begin. (You will need a sheet of paper to write your answers on.) When finished, turn back to this chapter and correct your test. The answers are in the same order as exercise II.

VII.) Write a sentence for each new word. Are you ready to use the new words? Write a sentence for each new word.

systemic	malignant	entrepreneur	entomologist	capricious
mutagen	caustic	precarious	emanating	flamboyant
defoliant	cascade	disseminate	metabolism	subsidiary

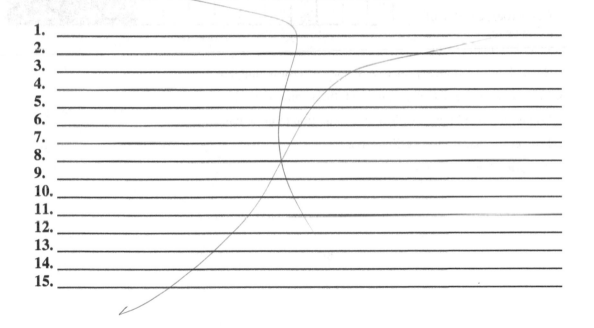

1. _____
2. _____
3. _____
4. _____
5. _____
6. _____
7. _____
8. _____
9. _____
10. _____
11. _____
12. _____
13. _____
14. _____
15. _____

VIII.) Your instructor may ask you to do the puzzle on the next page. It is the same as the one on your CD. You are able to do it here once or on the CD as many times as you'd like.

Across

1. A chemical used to destroy the leaves on plants.

4. Waterfall, series of waterfalls over tumbling over rocks.

8. Corrosive, able to eat away at metal and other substances, erosive.

9. A founder of a business venture.

10. Physical and chemical process that converts food to energy and is necessary for life and health.

Down

1. Spread, scatter, diffuse, strew, distribute.

2. Cancerous, capable of causing death, lie-threatening, malevolent.

3. Second in importance, franchise, branch, division, unit, auxiliary.

4. Impulsive, unpredictable, whimsical, fickle, unpredictable.

5. Something that induces or increases mutation in an organism.

6. Dangerous, hazardous, perilous, risky.

7. Affecting the entire body

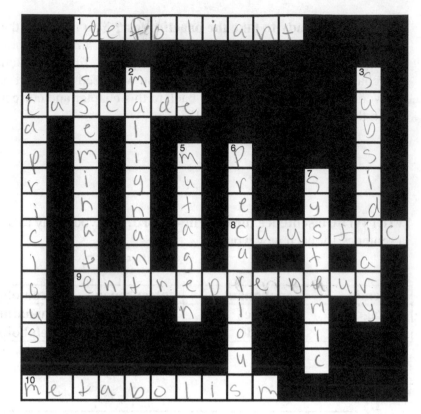

Rewrite your words/Practice Test

New word: **Practice writing the new word:**

Rewrite your words/Practice test

New word:	Practice writing the new word:		

Advancing College Vocabulary & Spelling Skills

I.) *Use context to arrive at meaning.* **Complete the following sentences with words that are familiar to you and that make sense in each sentence. You may write more than one word choice for each blank space. <u>Do not</u> look at or study the new words yet. Answers will vary and your instructor will discuss them with you.**

Contemptuous
esteemed
deliberation
presumptuous
effectual
avaricious
rapacious
Lascivious
parsimony
Stimulators
Justification
Patrimony
allegory

anarchy
irresolute

1. The King acted in a very _rude / deceitful_ manner, often treating his subjects disrespectfully.
2. Princess Diana was greatly _acknowledged_ by the public for her many charitable acts.
3. The _People_ of the jury lasted four days as they considered all of the evidence.
4. A person probably would be too _disrespectful_ if they entered your home without knocking first.
5. The medicine proved to be very _affective_; it cured the patient in just three days.
6. Luke was said to be very _entitled_ in his quest for wealth; no amount of money seemed to be enough.
7. The tyrant's _fierce_ attitude moved him to plunder the conquered lands.
8. The _entrigued_ actions of the people led to many lustful actions.
9. His _selfish_ attitude led to his hoarding the wealth of the Nation for his own use, while the people lived in poverty.
10. The court officials tended to be _imitators_ of the evil ruler by imitating his actions.
11. Often people will seek a _angel_ in their minds to try to defend their evil deeds.
12. The government should not interfere with a person's _property_ that is left to them by an estate.
13. A story that is told in order to teach a moral lesson is called a(n) _parble_.
14. A lack of governmental control often produces _Chaos_.
15. James was very _Confused_ because he did not know what to do next.

II.)   ***Study the words and definitions below.*** These words and definitions are also on the enclosed CD Rom and may be printed out as study cards. The words are broken into letter groupings for easier spelling. Also, that is followed by a common definition, and common forms of the word that you might encounter. Your instructor will pronounce the words for you or you may want to use an audio dictionary for more help.

1.   **contemptuous:** (con/temp/tu/ous) Having a scornful, disrespectful attitude towards others. Also: **contemptuously, contemptuousness.**
2.   **esteem:** (es/teem) To hold in high regard, to hold in an honored position. Also: **esteemed, esteeming, esteems.**
3.   **deliberation:** (de/lib/er/a/tion) To discuss and evaluate many sides of an issue. Also: **deliberations.**
4.   **presumptuous:** (pre/sump/tu/ous) Going beyond what is considered proper, being too forward. Also: **presumptuously, presumptuousness.**
5.   **effectual:** (e/ff/ect/ual) Producing, or able to produce, the desired effect. Also: **effectuality, effectualness, effectually.**
6.   **avaricious:** (a/var/i/ci/ous) Greedy, lusting for wealth or other gain. Also: **avariciously, avariciousness.**
7.   **rapacious:** (ra/pa/ci/ous) Plundering, seizing. Also: **rapaciously, rapacity, rapaciousness.**
8.   **lascivious:** (las/civ/i/ous) lustful. Also: **lasciviously, lasciviousness.**
9.   **parsimony:** (par/si/mony) Extremely stingy or frugal; penny-pinching. Also: **parsimonious**
10. **simulators:** (sim/u/la/tors) Those who imitate some person especially as a means of winning favor or position.
11. **justify:** (jus/ti/fy) To provide reasons for an action that will excuse, ease, or placate the conscience; rationalize; substantiate; defend. Also: **justification, justified, justifying, justifies.**
12. **patrimony:** (pa/tri/mony) An inheritance from a father (patri) or other ancestor. Also: **patrimonial.**
13. **allegory:** (all/e/gory) Using a story or symbol to represent deeper concepts, meanings, truths, or principles. Also: **allegorically, allegorical, allegories, allegorist.**
14. **anarchy:** (an/ar/chy) Lawlessness, no governmental control, political disorder. Also: **anarchist, anarchism, anarchistic.**
15. **irresolute:** (irr/es/o/lute) or (ir/res/o/lute) Indecisive; not sure of how to proceed. Also: **irresolutely, irresoluteness, irresolution.**

III.) ***Match the words with their definitions.*** Draw a line connecting each word with its correct definition.

1. contemptuous		a. indecisive
2. irresolute		b. highly regarded
3. rapacious		c. stingy
4. avaricious		d. rationalize
5. esteemed		e. imitators
6. lascivious		f. story
7. parsimony		g. scornful
8. deliberations		h. plundering
9. anarchy		i. lustful
10. allegory		j. political disorder
11. patrimony		k. discussions
12. justify		l. inheritance
13. presumptuous		m. too forward
14. effectual		n. greedy
15. simulators		o. workable

IV.) ***Puzzle work.*** Now try the interactive puzzle. Put the CD (that came with your workbook) into the computer, and work the puzzle. A paper copy of the puzzle is also included at the end of this chapter.

V.)   Write the correct new word in each sentence below:

contemptuous	irresolute	rapacious	simulators	allegory
effectual	presumptuous	justify	patrimony	esteemed
anarchy	deliberations	parsimony	lascivious	avaricious

1. The King acted in a very _contemptuous_ manner, often treating his subjects disrespectfully.
2. Princess Diana was greatly _esteemed_ by the public for her many charitable acts.
3. The _deliberation_ of the jury lasted four days as they considered all of the evidence.
4. A person probably would be too _presumptuous_ if they entered your home without knocking first.
5. The medicine proved to be very _effectual_; it cured the patient in just three days.
6. Luke was said to be very _avaricious_ in his quest for wealth; no amount of money seemed to be enough.
7. The tyrant's _rapacious_ attitude moved him to plunder the conquered lands.
8. The _lascivious_ actions of the people led to many lustful actions.
9. His _parsimony_ attitude led to his hoarding the wealth of the Nation for his own use, while the people lived in poverty.
10. The court officials tended to be _simulators_ of the evil ruler by imitating his actions.
11. Often people will seek a _justification_ in their minds to try to defend their evil deeds.
12. The government should not interfere with a person's _patrimony_ that is left to them by an estate.
13. A story that is told in order to teach a moral lesson is called a(n) _allegory_.
14. A lack of governmental control often produces _anarchy_.
15. James was very _irresolute_ because he did not know what to do next.

VI.) Are you ready to take the practice test? You may take the practice test as many times as you want to. Simply insert the CD that came with book into your computer, go to "My Computer", open the CD by clicking on it, find the Practice test folder, choose this chapter's practice test and begin. (You will need a sheet of paper to write your answers on.) When finished, turn back to this chapter and correct your test. The answers are in the same order as exercise II.

VII.) Write a sentence for each new word. Are you ready to use the new words? Write a sentence for each new word.

contemptuous	irresolute	rapacious	simulators	allegory
effectual	presumptuous	justify	patrimony	esteemed
anarchy	deliberations	parsimony	lascivious	avaricious

1. _____
2. _____
3. _____
4. _____
5. _____
6. _____
7. _____
8. _____
9. _____
10. _____
11. _____
12. _____
13. _____
14. _____
15. _____

VIII.) Your instructor may ask you to do the puzzle on the next page. It is the same as the one on your CD. You are able to do it here once or on the CD as many times as you'd like.

Across

2. To hold in high regard

4. To provide reasons for an action that will excuse, ease, or placate the conscience; rationalize; substantiate; defend.

6. Indecisive; not sure of how to proceed.

8. Greedy, lusting for wealth or other gain.

9. Plundering, seizing.

10. Having a scornful, disrespectful attitude towards others.

11. Producing, or able to produce, the desired effect.

Down

1. To discuss and evaluate many sides of an issue.

3. Lustful

5. Going beyond what is considered proper, being too forward.

7. An inheritance

8. Lawlessness, no governmental control, political disorder

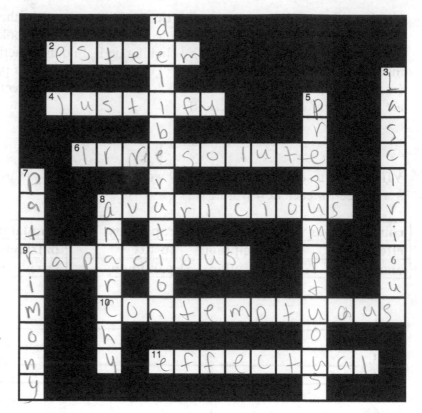

Rewrite your words/Practice Test

New word:		Practice writing the new word:	

Rewrite your words/Practice test

New word:		Practice writing the new word:	

Advancing College Vocabulary & Spelling Skills

I.)   **Use context to arrive at meaning.** Complete the following sentences with words that are familiar to you and that make sense in each sentence. You may write more than one word choice for each blank space. <u>Do not</u> look at or study the new words yet. Answers will vary and your instructor will discuss them with you.

(handwritten words in left margin):
Ununimous
Impelled
Inalienable
principles
transient
usurped
invariably
evinces
despot
constrained
tyranny
inestimable
formidable
appropriations
tenure

1.   The vote was _____ *passed* _____ and all Senators were in favor of tax relief.
2.   The delegates were _____ *eager* _____ to take action after the terrorist attack.
3.   It is every American's _____ *legal* _____ right to have freedom.
4.   The underlying _____ *truth* _____ of a good government provide for the well being of the citizens of that country.
5.   The homeless person was always just "passing through" and was therefore labeled a _____ *bum* _____.
6.   History provides us with many accounts of persons who have _____ *ultimate* power by taking that which did not belong to them.
7.   _____, we know that there will always be strife on planet Earth.
8.   Bad conduct clearly _____ *shows* _____ bad morals.
9.   The _____ *leader* _____ ruled with an iron fist.
10. The people felt _____ *used* _____ by the dictator and   ultimately they rebelled.
11. Living under _____ *constitution*, where the people have few rights, is still a problem in our world today.
12. The number who died in the deadly earthquake was a(n) _____ *high* _____ number since many bodies were not able to be recovered or counted.
13. Germany was a _____ *strong* _____ foe during WW II and was not easily defeated.
14. The British king did not allow for new land _____ *settlements* therefore the settlers had no new land to settle onto.
15. When an instructor receives _____ *tenure* _____ he/she no longer has to renew the teaching contract each year.

II.)   *Study the words and definitions below.* These words and definitions are also on the enclosed CD Rom and may be printed out as study cards. The words are broken into letter groupings for easier spelling. Also, that is followed by a common definition, and common forms of the word that you might encounter. Your instructor will pronounce the words for you or you may want to use an audio dictionary for more help.

1. **unanimous** (u/nan/i/mous) Being in total agreement, 100% in harmony or assent, complete accord, of one mind. Also: **unanimously.**
2. **impel** (impel) To urge into action, to push forward. Also: **impelled, impelling, impels.**
3. **inalienable** (in/al/i/en/ab/le or in/alien/able) not able to be foreign to, clear, without misunderstanding (in =not, alien= foreign, able=able to – not able to be foreign to). Also: **inalienability, inalienably.**
4. **principle** (prin/ci/ple) a moral standard, a truth, a norm for good conduct.
5. **transient** (tran/si/ent) fleeting, remaining for only a brief time, short-lived. Also: **transiently.**
6. **usurp** (u/surp) to take by force that which is not rightfully yours. Also: **usurper, usurpations, usurped, usurping, usurps.**
7. **invariably** (in/var/ia/bly) Not subject to change, constant (in=not, variable=change, able=able to – not able to change) . Also: **invariableness, invariably, invariability.**
8. **evince** (e/vin/ce) To clearly manifest, demonstrate, or show. Also: **evinces, evincible, evinced, evincing.**
9. **despot** (des/pot) A tyrant, an evil ruler with total power. Also: **despotic, despotism, despotically.**
10. **constrain** (con/st/rain) to have pressure to act; to produce under pressure; to hold back. Also: **constrains, constrained, constrainable, constrainer.**
11. **tyrant** (ty/rant) a dictator; one who rules with an iron fist, an oppressive person. Also: **tyranny, tyrannical.**
12. **inestimable** (in/es/ti/ma/ble) Not able to put a number on. (in=not, estimate=wisely guess at, able= able to – not able to estimate or within reason give a number.) Also: **inestimably.**
13. **formidable** (form/i/da/ble) difficult to defeat; strong; dreadful. Also: **formidableness, formidability, formidably.**
14. **appropriate** (a/pp/ro/pria/te or ap/pro/pria/te) To set aside such as funds or land for a specific use. Also: **appropriation, appropriated, appropriating, appropriates.**
15. **tenure** (ten/ure) Time during which something is held (a job, a political office, etc.); holding on a permanent basis without the need for contract renewals.

III.) *Match the words with their definitions.* Draw a line connecting each word with its correct definition.

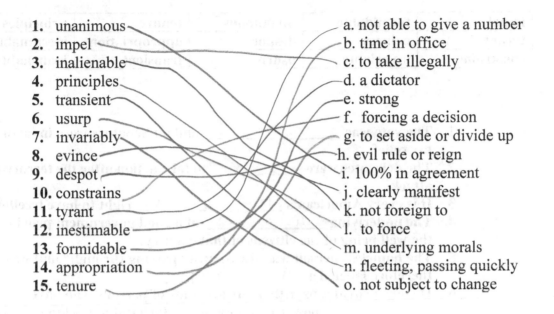

1. unanimous
2. impel
3. inalienable
4. principles
5. transient
6. usurp
7. invariably
8. evince
9. despot
10. constrains
11. tyrant
12. inestimable
13. formidable
14. appropriation
15. tenure

a. not able to give a number
b. time in office
c. to take illegally
d. a dictator
e. strong
f. forcing a decision
g. to set aside or divide up
h. evil rule or reign
i. 100% in agreement
j. clearly manifest
k. not foreign to
l. to force
m. underlying morals
n. fleeting, passing quickly
o. not subject to change

IV.) *Puzzle work.* Now try the interactive puzzle. Put the CD (that came with your workbook) into the computer, and work the puzzle. A paper copy of the puzzle is also included at the end of this chapter.

V.)   **Write the correct new word in each sentence below:**

impel	formidable	unanimous	tenure	principles
tyrant	evinces	despot	appropriation	inestimable
constrains	invariably	usurp	transient	inalienable

1. The vote was ___Unanimous___ and all Senators were in favor of tax relief.
2. The delegates were ___Impelled___ to take action after the terrorist attack.
3. It is every American's ___inalienable___ right to have freedom.
4. The underlying ___Principles___ of a good government provide for the well being of the citizens of that country.
5. The homeless person was always just "passing through" and was therefore labeled a ___transient___.
6. History provides us with many accounts of persons who have ___usurped___ power by taking that which did not belong to them.
7. ___Invariably___, we know that there will always be strife on planet Earth.
8. Bad conduct clearly ___evinces___ bad morals.
9. The ___despot___ ruled with an iron fist.
10. The people felt ___constrained___ by the dictator and ultimately they rebelled.
11. Living under ___tyranny___, where the people have few rights, is still a problem in our world today.
12. The number who died in the deadly earthquake was a(n) ___inestimable___ number since many bodies were not able to be recovered or counted.
13. Germany was a ___formidable___ foe during WW II and was not easily defeated.
14. The British king did not allow for new land ___appropriations___ therefore the settlers had no new land to settle onto.
15. When an instructor receives ___tenure___ he/she no longer has to renew the teaching contract each year.

VI.) Are you ready to take the practice test? You may take the practice test as many times as you want to.   Simply insert the CD that came with book into your computer, go to "My Computer", open the CD by clicking on it, find the Practice test folder, choose this chapter's practice test and begin. (You will need a sheet of paper to write your answers on.) When finished, turn back to this chapter and correct your test. The answers are in the same order as exercise II.

VII.) Write a sentence for each new word. Are you ready to use the new words? Write a sentence for each new word.

impel	formidable	unanimous	tenure	principles
tyrant	evinces	despot	appropriation	inestimable
constrains	invariably	usurp	transient	inalienable

1. _____
2. _____
3. _____
4. _____
5. _____
6. _____
7. _____
8. _____
9. _____
10. _____
11. _____
12. _____
13. _____
14. _____
15. _____

VIII.) Your instructor may ask you to do the puzzle on the next page. It is the same as the one on your CD. You are able to do it here once or on the CD as many times as you'd like.

Across

2. Being in total agreement, 100% in harmony or assent, complete accord, of one mind.

6. Time during which something is held (a job, a political office, etc); holding on a permanent basis without the need for contract renewals.

8. Fleeting, remaining for only a brief time, short-lived.

9. To set aside such as funds or land for a specific use.

12. To clearly manifest, demonstrate, or show.

13. A moral standard, a truth, a norm for good conduct.

14. Not able to put a number on.

Down

1. A dictator; one who rules with an iron fist, an oppressive person.

3. Not able to be foreign to, clear, without misunderstanding

4. To take by force that which is not rightfully yours.

5. Not subject to change, constant

7. To have pressure to act; to produce under pressure; to hold back.

10. A tyrant, an evil ruler with total power.

11. To urge into action, to push forward.

Rewrite your words/Practice Test

New word: **Practice writing the new word:**

Rewrite your words/Practice test

New word: **Practice writing the new word:**

Advancing College Vocabulary & Spelling Skills

I.)   *Use context to arrive at meaning.* **Complete the following sentences with words that are familiar to you and that make sense in each sentence. You may write more than one word choice for each blank space. <u>Do not</u> look at or study the new words yet. Answers will vary and your instructor will discuss them with you.**

1.   The judge's decision was considered very _____ because he made his decision based on the defendant's appearance.
2.   A dictator has _____ control over the country.
3.   The Congress is _____ with certain powers as granted by our Constitution.
4.   His sudden illness forced him to _____ his Senate seat.
5.   The _____ of such an action – shaking the Governor's hand and then shooting him.
6.   There were many _____ against the government because of its repressive policies.
7.   After the war, the people sought _____ for the manner in which they had been treated.
8.   Those actions are without provocation; they are _____.
9.   Each Governor has _____ over his/her own state.
10. She has a _____ manner because she has always been unselfish, forgiving and noble.
11. He _____ any previous knowledge or connection with the terrorist group.
12. Having recently emigrated from Great Britain, the colonists felt great _____ with them.
13. Even though many did not like the new laws, most _____ to them.
14. The group's intentions showed great _____ and their moral excellence was evident to all.
15. The evil actions showed the _____ intent of the king.

II.)   *Study the words and definitions below.* These words and definitions are also on the enclosed CD Rom and may be printed out as study cards. The words are broken into letter groupings for easier spelling. Also, that is followed by a common definition, and common forms of the word that you might encounter. Your instructor will pronounce the words for you or you may want to use an audio dictionary for more help.

1. **arbitrary** (ar/bi/tr/ary) without rule or reason; not according to laws or standards. Also: **arbitrarily, arbitrariness**.
2. **absolute** (ab/so/lute) Without limitations, complete and final authority.
3. **invest** (in/vest) Give appropriate power or legal authority. Also: **invested, investing, invests**.
4. **abdicate** (ab/di/ca/te) To give up a position or office. Also: **abdicated, abdication, abdicator**.
5. **perfidy** (per/fidy) A breach of trust; treason; treachery.
6. **insurrection** (in/surr/ec/tion) An uprising of the people against the government. Also: **insurrectionism, insurrectionist, insurrectionary, insurrectional**.
7. **redress** (re/dress) to remedy a situation through making amends; rectify; reparation. Also: **redressed, redressing, redresses**.
8. **unwarrantable** (un/warr/ant/a/ble or un/warr/ant/able) not justifiable, without excuse (un = not, warrant = justification, able = able to – not able to justify) Also: **unwarranted, unwarrantably**.
9. **jurisdiction** (jur/is/dic/tion) The authority or control over an area. Also: **jurisdictional, jurisdictionally**.
10. **magnanimous** (mag/nan/i/mous) Generous; noble in character, unselfishness. (the prefix magn = great, huge) Also: **magnanimity, magnanimously, magnanimousness**.
11. **disavow** (dis/a/vow) to claim that one has no prior knowledge, association or ties to something or someone. Also: **disavowal, disavowed**.
12. **consanguinity** (con/san/guin/ity) Relationship by common ancestry or other close connection. Also: **consanguinities**.
13. **acquiesce** (ac/qui/es/ce) To give in to another's wishes without protest. Also: **acquiesced, acquiescing, acquiesces**.
14. **rectitude** (rec/ti/tude) Moral uprightness, honesty, fair and correct in judgment.
15. **barbarous** (bar/bar/ous) Uncivilized, savage, beast-like, cruel. Also: **barbarously**.

III.) ***Match the words with their definitions.*** Draw a line connecting each word with its correct definition.

1. arbitrary		a. to give in
2. absolute		b. uncivilized
3. invested		c. close ties as by relationship
4. abdicate		d. reparations
5. perfidy		e. uprisings
6. barbarous		f. to claim no connection to
7. insurrections		g. territory governed over
8. redress		h. without proper judgment
9. unwarrantable		i. unquestioned
10. jurisdiction		j. has legal authority
11. magnanimous		k. to give up rule or position
12. disavow		l. treason
13. consanguinity		m. without good reasons
14. acquiesce		n. noble in character
15. rectitude		o. moral uprightness

IV.) ***Puzzle work.*** Now try the interactive puzzle. Put the CD (that came with your workbook) into the computer, and work the puzzle. A paper copy of the puzzle is also included at the end of this chapter.

V.)   Write the correct new word in each sentence below:

perfidy	barbarous	arbitrary	disavow	rectitude
acquiesce	redress	jurisdiction	magnanimous	insurrections
absolute	consanguinity	invest	unwarrantable	abdicated

1. The judge's decision was considered very _____ because he made his decision based on the defendant's appearance.
2. A dictator has _____ control over the country.
3. The Congress is _____ with certain powers as granted by our Constitution.
4. His sudden illness forced him to _____ his Senate seat.
5. The _____ of such an action – shaking the Governor's hand and then shooting him.
6. There were many _____ against the government because of its repressive policies.
7. After the war, the people sought _____ for the manner in which they had been treated.
8. Those actions are without provocation; they are _____.
9. Each Governor has _____ over his/her own state.
10. She has a _____ manner because she has always been unselfish, forgiving and noble.
11. He _____ any previous knowledge or connection with the terrorist group.
12. Having recently emigrated from Great Britain, the colonists felt great _____ with them.
13. Even though many did not like the new laws, most _____ to them.
14. The group's intentions showed great _____ and their moral excellence was evident to all.
15. The evil actions showed the _____ intent of the king.

VI.) Are you ready to take the practice test? You may take the practice test as many times as you want to. Simply insert the CD that came with book into your computer, go to "My Computer", open the CD by clicking on it, find the Practice test folder, choose this chapter's practice test and begin. (You will need a sheet of paper to write your answers on.) When finished, turn back to this chapter and correct your test. The answers are in the same order as exercise II.

VII.) Write a sentence for each new word. Are you ready to use the new words? Write a sentence for each new word.

perfidy	barbarous	arbitrary	disavow	rectitude
acquiesce	redress	jurisdiction	magnanimous	insurrections
absolute	consanguinity	invest	unwarrantable	abdicated

1. _____
2. _____
3. _____
4. _____
5. _____
6. _____
7. _____
8. _____
9. _____
10. _____
11. _____
12. _____
13. _____
14. _____
15. _____

VIII.) Your instructor may ask you to do the puzzle on the next page. It is the same as the one on your CD. You are able to do it here once or on the CD as many times as you'd like.

Across

1. Not justifiable, without excuse

6. Without rule or reason; not according to laws or standards

10. To remedy a situation through making amends; rectify; reparation

11. Give appropriate power or legal authority.

12. Generous; noble in character, unselfishness.

13. An uprising of people against the government.

Down

2. To give in to another's wishes without protest.

3. Uncivilized, savage, beast-like, cruel

4. A breach of trust; treason; treachery

5. The authority or control over an area.

7. To claim that one has no prior knowledge, association or ties to something or someone.

8. Moral uprightness, honesty, fair and correct in judgment.

9. To give up a position or office.

Rewrite your words/Practice Test

New word: **Practice writing the new word:**

Rewrite your words/Practice test

New word:		Practice writing the new word:	

Advancing College Vocabulary & Spelling Skills

I.) Use context to arrive at meaning. Complete the following sentences with words that are familiar to you and that make sense in each sentence. You may write more than one word choice for each blank space. <u>Do not</u> look at or study the new words yet. Answers will vary and your instructor will discuss them with you.

1. I consider myself part of the _____ class since I own an automobile, have a job, and live comfortably.
2. Generally speaking, people who do not have a degree, have a more difficult time economically and are considered part of the _____ class of society.
3. In what _____ of history did Dolly Madison live?
4. People often _____ higher taxes.
5. In the movie "The Exorcist," a priest tried to _____ the demon out of the possessed girl.
6. Karl is a very _____ person who always wants revenge when he feels mistreated.
7. Rosalie is considered the _____ of her family due to her strength and leadership.
8. Miguel's transcript shows A's in nearly every class. That is a very _____ accomplishment.
9. The two hostile groups showed a lot of _____ towards each other.
10. The _____ group was opposed to any progress.
11. The founders of the United States stated a reliance on Divine _____.
12. Higher taxes by the state tended to _____ any benefit that the federal tax gave the citizens.
13. The _____ class of kings, queens and nobility felt that the peasants were an inferior class of citizens.
14. The _____ of another storm following the first instilled fear in the population.
15. Mr. Ramirez was considered a kind _____ by his family since he provided well for every member and was a fine example of moral leadership.

73

II.)   *Study the words and definitions below.* These words and definitions are also on the enclosed CD Rom and may be printed out as study cards. The words are broken into letter groupings for easier spelling. Also, that is followed by a common definition, and common forms of the word that you might encounter. Your instructor will pronounce the words for you or you may want to use an audio dictionary for more help.

1. **bourgeois** (bour/geo/is) A middle-class person; in Marxist theory, a property owner or capitalist.

2. **proletariat** (pro/le/tar/iat) Industrial wage earners; poorest class; lowest class. Also: **proletarian, proletarianism**

3. **patrician** (pa/tri/cian) upper class, elite, highborn, aristocrat.

4. **exorcise** (ex/or/cise) to release from evil spirits or demons. Also: **exorcism, exorcist.**

5. **reactionary** (re/ac/tion/ary) extremely opposed to progress.

6. **laudable** (laud/a/ble) worthy of praise.

7. **decry** (de/cry) to openly condemn. Also: **decried, decrying, decries.**

8. **specter** (spec/ter) a haunting or very disturbing prediction; a ghostly or eerie threat.

9. **epoch** (e/poch) a particular time or place in history, a period of time.

10. **vindictive** (vin/dic/tive) bearing a grudge, inclined towards revenge, revengeful.

11. **Providence** (Prov/i/dence) God; divine guidance. Also: **providential.**

12. **antagonism** (an/ta/gon/ism) opposition, defiance, resistance. Also: **antagonist, antagonize.**

13. **negate** (ne/gate) to end, cancel, void, make ineffective.

14. **patriarch** (pa/tri/ar/ch) A man who rules the family; position of authority in many religions; an elder; an old venerated man. Also: **patriarchal, patriarchic, patriarchalism, patriarchally.**

15. **matriarch** (ma/tri/arch) A woman who rules the family; highly respected mother; a woman who dominates, and is respected by a group. Also: **matriarchal, matriarchic, matriarchalism.**

III.) *Match the words with their definitions.* Draw a line connecting each word with its correct definition.

1. bourgeois	a. woman who rules the family
2. proletariat	b. divine guidance
3. patrician	c. a historical period
4. exorcise	d. resistance
5. reactionary	e. to cancel
6. laudable	f. upper class
7. decry	g. disturbing prediction
8. specter	h. a man who rules his family
9. epoch	i. condemn
10. vindictive	j. extremely opposed to progress
11. Providence	k. worthy of praise
12. antagonism	l. middle class person
13. negate	m. lowest class in society
14. patriarch	n. release from evil spirits
15. matriarch	o. inclined towards revenge

IV.) *Puzzle work.* Now try the interactive puzzle. Put the CD (that came with your workbook) into the computer, and work the puzzle. A paper copy of the puzzle is also included at the end of this chapter.

V.)   Write the correct new word in each sentence below:

epoch	decry	negate	specter	bourgeois
proletariat	vindictive	antagonism	reactionary	patriarch
patrician	laudable	matriarch	exorcise	Providence

1. I consider myself part of the _____ class since I own an automobile, have a job, and live comfortably.
2. Generally speaking, people who do not have a degree, have a more difficult time economically and are considered part of the _____ class of society.
3. In what _____ of history did Dolly Madison live?
4. People often _____ higher taxes.
5. In the movie "The Exorcist," a priest tried to _____ the demon out of the possessed girl.
6. Karl is a very _____ person who always wants revenge when he feels mistreated.
7. Rosalie is considered the _____ of her family due to her strength and leadership.
8. Miguel's transcript shows A's in nearly every class. That is a very _____ accomplishment.
9. The two hostile groups showed a lot of _____ towards each other.
10. The _____ group was opposed to any progress.
11. The founders of the United States stated a reliance on Divine _____.
12. Higher taxes by the state tended to _____ any benefit that the federal tax gave the citizens.
13. The _____ class of kings, queens and nobility felt that the peasants were an inferior class of citizens.
14. The _____ of another storm following the first instilled fear in the population.
15. Mr. Ramirez was considered a kind _____ by his family since he provided well for every member and was a fine example of moral leadership.

VI.) Are you ready to take the practice test? You may take the practice test as many times as you want to.   Simply insert the CD that came with book into your computer, go to "My Computer", open the CD by clicking on it, find the Practice test folder, choose this chapter's practice test and begin. (You will need a sheet of paper to write your answers on.) When finished, turn back to this chapter and correct your test. The answers are in the same order as exercise II.

VII.) Write a sentence for each new word. Are you ready to use the new words? Write a sentence for each new word.

epoch	decry	negate	specter	bourgeois
proletariat	vindictive	antagonism	reactionary	patriarch
patrician	laudable	matriarch	exorcise	Providence

1. _____
2. _____
3. _____
4. _____
5. _____
6. _____
7. _____
8. _____
9. _____
10. _____
11. _____
12. _____
13. _____
14. _____
15. _____

VIII.) Your instructor may ask you to do the puzzle on the next page. It is the same as the one on your CD. You are able to do it here once or on the CD as many times as you'd like.

Across

3. Defiance, opposition

5. To openly condemn

6. Revered older man

9. Revengeful

10. Middle-class person

11. Cancel out

12. Extremely opposed to progress

Down

1. Worthy of praise

2. Upper class, elite

4. Period in history

6. Divine guidance

7. Revered older woman

8. Disturbing prediction

78

Rewrite your words/Practice Test

New word:		Practice writing the new word:		

Rewrite your words/Practice test

New word:		Practice writing the new word:		

Advancing College Vocabulary & Spelling Skills

I.) Use context to arrive at meaning. Complete the following sentences with words that are familiar to you and that make sense in each sentence. You may write more than one word choice for each blank space. <u>Do not</u> look at or study the new words yet. Answers will vary and your instructor will discuss them with you.

1. Some oils and fats tend to _____ in the bloodstream.
2. The Iroquois Indians were _____ to the state of New York since their ancestry was well established in that area over hundreds of years.
3. The enemy decided to _____ to the soldier's request.
4. The _____ that I felt, when I discovered that I had on two different colored shoes, was almost unbearable.
5. A donkey is a very _____ creature.
6. Christy has a very _____ view of the world since her employment with United Airlines has allowed her to travel all over the globe.
7. The _____ felt by all of the Gold medal winners was awesome.
8. Larry had a(n) _____ that something bad would happen that day, and he later had a car accident.
9. Karl has a very _____ attitude since he only thinks about how great he is.
10. The captives were held in _____ until their trials.
11. Some people have a very _____ way of seeing the world, but I prefer a more realistic view.
12. Every United States citizen has a(n) _____ right to a fair trial.
13. The _____ old man was a model citizen in his hometown.
14. The lava began to _____ as it cooled.
15. The killing of innocent people is a(n) _____ act that many would find almost impossible to forgive.

II.)   ***Study the words and definitions below.*** These words and definitions are also on the enclosed CD Rom and may be printed out as study cards. The words are broken into letter groupings for easier spelling. Also, that is followed by a common definition, and common forms of the word that you might encounter. Your instructor will pronounce the words for you or you may want to use an audio dictionary for more help.

1. **agglomerate** (agg/lom/er/ate) to collect or form into a circular mass; to increase mass by uniting. Also: **agglomerated, agglomerating, agglomerates, agglomeration.**
2. **capitulate** (ca/pi/tu/late) to yield, to submit, to surrender to another's wishes. Also: **capitulation, capitulant, capitulator, capitulated, capitulating, capitulates.**
3. **chagrin** (cha/grin) mental uneasiness, embarrassment. Also: **chagrined, chagrins, chagrining.**
4. **cosmopolitan** (cos/mo/pol/i/tan) concerning the entire world. Also: **cosmopolitanism.**
5. **ecstasies** (ecs/tas/ies) intense feeling of joy, happiness, delight, elation. Also: **ecstasy.**
6. **egotistical** (e/go/tis/ti/cal) in the manner of being conceited, boastful or self-centered. Also: **egotist, egotistic, egotistically.**
7. **fetters** (fe/tt/ers) chains, restrictions, hindrances. Also: fetter, fettered, fettering.
8. **idyllic** (i/dy/ll/ic) simple, tranquil, carefree. Also: idyll, idyllist.
9. **indefeasible** (in/de/feas/ible) cannot be made void or annulled. Also: **indefeasibility, indefeasibly.**
10. **indigenous** (in/di/gen/ous) native, of a certain area or environment; by birth or origin. Also: **indigenously, indigenousness.**
11. **obstinate** (ob/stin/ate) stubbornly sticking to an opinion, attitude, or series of actions. Also: **obstinately, obstinateness.**
12. **ossify** (oss/i/fy) to make solid, to set rigidly, fossilize, turn to stone. Also: ossified, ossifying, ossifies.
13. **presentiment** (pre/sen/ti/ment) premonition, sense that something is about to happen. Also: **presentimental**
14. **unconscionable** (un/con/scion/able) unscrupulous, not restrained by feelings of guilt, not bothered by conscience, dishonorable, immoral. Also: **unconscionably, unconscionableness.**
15. **venerable** (ven/er/able) worthy of respect or reverence, old and revered. Also: **venerably, venerability, venerableness.**

III.) *Match the words with their definitions.* Draw a line connecting each word with its correct definition.

1.	agglomerate	a. tranquil
2.	capitulate	b. intense joy
3.	chagrin	c. restrictions
4.	cosmopolitan	d. concerning the entire world
5.	ecstasies	e. stubborn
6.	egotistical	f. to yield
7.	fetters	g. revered
8.	idyllic	h. boastful
9.	indefeasible	i. embarrass
10.	indigenous	j. solidify
11.	obstinate	k. premonition
12.	ossify	l. not bothered by conscience
13.	presentiment	m. native to an area
14.	unconscionable	n. form into circular mass
15.	venerable	o. cannot be made void

IV.) *Puzzle work.* Now try the interactive puzzle. Put the CD (that came with your workbook) into the computer, and work the puzzle. A paper copy of the puzzle is also included at the end of this chapter.

V.)   Write the correct new word in each sentence below:

ossify	fetters	idyllic	indefeasible	venerable
capitulate	egotistical	presentiment	unconscionable	ecstasies
indigenous	obstinate	agglomerate	chagrin	cosmopolitan

1. Some oils and fats tend to _____ in the bloodstream.
2. The Iroquois Indians were _____ to the state of New York since their ancestry was well established in that area over hundreds of years.
3. The enemy decided to _____ to the soldier's request.
4. The _____ that I felt, when I discovered that I had on two different colored shoes, was almost unbearable.
5. A donkey is a very _____ creature.
6. Christy has a very _____ view of the world since her employment with United Airlines has allowed her to travel all over the globe.
7. The _____ felt by all of the Gold medal winners was awesome.
8. Larry had a _____ that something bad would happen that day, and he later had a car accident.
9. Karl has a very _____ attitude since he only thinks about how great he is.
10. The captives were held in _____ until their trials.
11. Some people have a very _____ way of seeing the world, but I prefer a more realistic view.
12. Every United States citizen has a(n) _____ right to a fair trial.
13. The _____ old man was a model citizen in his hometown.
14. The lava began to _____ as it cooled.
15. The killing of innocent people is an _____ act that many would find almost impossible to forgive.

VI.) Are you ready to take the practice test? You may take the practice test as many times as you want to. Simply insert the CD that came with book into your computer, go to "My Computer", open the CD by clicking on it, find the Practice test folder, choose this chapter's practice test and begin. (You will need a sheet of paper to write your answers on.) When finished, turn back to this chapter and correct your test. The answers are in the same order as exercise II.

VII.) Write a sentence for each new word. Are you ready to use the new words? Write a sentence for each new word.

ossify	fetters	idyllic	indefeasible	venerable
capitulate	egotistical	presentiment	unconscionable	ecstasies
indigenous	obstinate	agglomerate	chagrin	cosmopolitan

1. _____
2. _____
3. _____
4. _____
5. _____
6. _____
7. _____
8. _____
9. _____
10. _____
11. _____
12. _____
13. _____
14. _____
15. _____

VIII.) Your instructor may ask you to do the puzzle on the next page. It is the same as the one on your CD. You are able to do it here once or on the CD as many times as you'd like.

Across

2. Cannot be made void or annulled

4. To make solid, to set rigidly, fossilize, turn to stone.

5. To collect or form into a circular mass; to increase mass by uniting

9. Stubbornly sticking to an opinion, attitude, or series of actions

10. Worthy of respect or reverence, old and revered.

11. Unscrupulous, not restrained by feelings of guilt, not bothered by conscience, dishonorable, immoral.

Down

1. Native, of a certain area or environment; by birth or origin

2. Simple, tranquil, carefree.

3. Intense feeling of joy, happiness, delight, elation.

6. In the manner of being conceited, boastful or self-centered

7. To yield, to submit, to surrender to another's wishes.

8. Mental uneasiness, embarrassment.

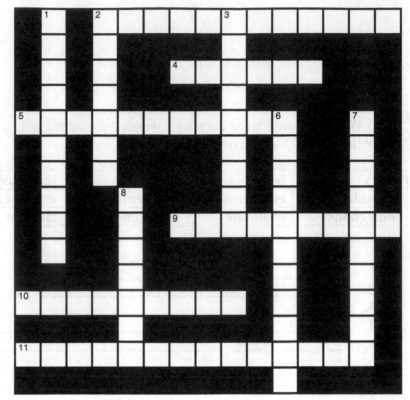

Rewrite your words/Practice Test

New word: **Practice writing the new word:**

Rewrite your words/Practice test

New word: **Practice writing the new word:**

Advancing College Vocabulary & Spelling Skills

I.)   Use context to arrive at meaning. Complete the following sentences with words that are familiar to you and that make sense in each sentence. You may write more than one word choice for each blank space. <u>Do not</u> look at or study the new words yet. Answers will vary and your instructor will discuss them with you.

1. Workers are often subjected to the _____ of competition and changing needs of the commercial world.
2. The _____ of rabbits, in the field behind our house, led us to believe that planting lettuce and carrots would not be wise.
3. The _____ of young woman by modeling agencies has to be stopped!
4. Do you think anything will _____ the Microsoft operating system?
5. According to some writers, the _____ region of the earth is inhabited by evil spirits.
6. Divorce can sometimes _____ a person.
7. She had to live on a meager _____ that hardly paid the bills.
8. His tone was very _____ and lulled me to sleep.
9. What _____ sells the best at that store?
10. The _____ conjured up a spell.
11. There are many _____ in the stock market.
12. His appendix burst _____.
13. Many people thought that the college hazing went too far and became _____.
14. Europe had a class system called _____ that kept many people in poverty and slave-like conditions.
15. The appendix is considered a(n) _____ to the human digestive tract.

II.) *Study the words and definitions below.* These words and definitions are also on the enclosed CD Rom and may be printed out as study cards. The words are broken into letter groupings for easier spelling. Also, that is followed by a common definition, and common forms of the word that you might encounter. Your instructor will pronounce the words for you or you may want to use an audio dictionary for more help.

1. **appendage** (app/en/dage) attachment, appendix, something added on.
2. **asunder (a/sun/der)** broken into separate parts or pieces.
3. **commodity** (comm/od/ity) a useful item that can be used commercially. Also: **commodities**
4. **embitter** (em/bitt/er) to make bitter (em = in, bitter = bitter: in a bitter manner) Also: **embittering, embittered, embitters.**
5. **exploitation** (ex/ploi/ta/tion) to take unfair advantage of.
6. **feudalism** (feu/dal/ism) a political system where an elite group controls the land and resources and everyone else is subservient to them. Also: **feudal, feudalist, feudalistic.**
7. **fluctuations:** (fluc/tua/tions) variations, irregular rise and fall. Also: **fluctuate, fluctuated, fluctuating, fluctuates.**
8. **monotonous** (mon/o/ton/ous) (mono = one, tonous = tone: one tone) spoken in one flat tone, repetitious, lacking variety. **Also: monotonously, monotonousness.**
9. **nether** (ne/ther) located beneath the earth; relating to hell.
10. **propagation** (pro/pa/ga/tion) spreading, multiplying, increasing. Also: **propagate, propagational.**
11. **repulsive** (re/pul/sive) disgusting, detestable, loathsome, disagreeable. Also: **repulsively, repulsiveness.**
12. **sorcerer** (sor/cer/er) one who uses supernatural powers; a wizard; a witch; conjurer of spells; warlock. Also: **sorceress** (female)**, sorcery.**
13. **subsistence** (sub/sis/tence) ability to support life, livelihood. Also: **subsistent.**
14. **supersede** (su/per/sede or super/sede) replace, take the place of, displace, oust, unseat, usurp. Also: **superseded, superseding, supersedes, superseder.**
15. **vicissitudes** (vi/ciss/i/tudes) changes, mutability. Also **vicissitude.**

III.) ***Match the words with their definitions.*** Draw a line connecting each word with its correct definition.

1.	appendage	a.	ability to support life
2.	asunder	b.	located beneath the earth
3.	commodity	c.	take advantage of
4.	embitter	d.	a conjurer of spells
5.	exploitation	e.	spreading
6.	feudalism	f.	to make bitter
7.	fluctuations	g.	one tone
8.	monotonous	h.	variations, irregular rise & fall
9.	nether	i.	class or caste like system
10.	propagation	j.	commercial item
11.	repulsive	k.	something added on
12.	sorcerer	l.	distasteful
13.	subsistence	m.	break into pieces
14.	supersede	n.	replace, usurp
15.	vicissitudes	o.	changes

IV.) ***Puzzle work.*** Now try the interactive puzzle. Put the CD (that came with your workbook) into the computer, and work the puzzle. A paper copy of the puzzle is also included at the end of this chapter.

V.)   Write the correct new word in each sentence below:

embitter	nether	supersede	vicissitudes	exploitation
propagation	subsistence	commodity	monotonous	repulsive
appendage	feudalism	sorcerer	fluctuations	asunder

1. Workers are often subjected to the _____ of competition and changing needs of the commercial world.
2. The _____ of rabbits, in the field behind our house, led us to believe that planting lettuce and carrots would not be wise.
3. The _____ of young woman by modeling agencies has to be stopped!
4. Do you think anything will _____ the Microsoft operating system?
5. According to some writers, the _____ region of the earth is inhabited by evil spirits.
6. Divorce can sometimes _____ a person.
7. She had to live on a meager _____ that hardly paid the bills.
8. His tone was very _____ and lulled me to sleep.
9. What _____ sells the best at that store?
10. The _____ conjured up a spell.
11. There are many _____ in the stock market.
12. His appendix burst _____.
13. Many people thought that the college hazing went too far and became _____.
14. Europe had a class system called _____ that kept many people in poverty and slave-like conditions.
15. The appendix is considered an _____ to the human digestive tract.

VI.) Are you ready to take the practice test? You may take the practice test as many times as you want to.   Simply insert the CD that came with book into your computer, go to "My Computer", open the CD by clicking on it, find the Practice test folder, choose this chapter's practice test and begin. (You will need a sheet of paper to write your answers on.) When finished, turn back to this chapter and correct your test. The answers are in the same order as exercise II.

VII.) Write a sentence for each new word. Are you ready to use the new words? Write a sentence for each new word.

embitter	nether	supersede	vicissitudes	exploitation
propagation	subsistence	commodity	monotonous	repulsive
appendage	feudalism	sorcerer	fluctuations	asunder

1. _____
2. _____
3. _____
4. _____
5. _____
6. _____
7. _____
8. _____
9. _____
10. _____
11. _____
12. _____
13. _____
14. _____
15. _____

VIII.) Your instructor may ask you to do the puzzle on the next page. It is the same as the one on your CD. You are able to do it here once or on the CD as many times as you'd like.

Across

3. Replace, take the place of, displace, oust, unseat, usurp.

4. Broken into separate parts or pieces.

8. A political system where an elite group controls the land and resources and everyone else is subservient to them

9. To make bitter

10. Spreading, multiplying, increasing.

11. Variations, irregular rise and fall.

Down

1. Attachment, appendix, something added on.

2. Disgusting, detestable, loathsome, disagreeable

3. One who uses supernatural powers; a wizard; a witch; conjurer of spells; warlock.

5. To take unfair advantage of.

6. Located beneath the earth; relating to hell

7. Spoken in one flat tone, repetitious, lacking variety.

Rewrite your words/Practice Test

New word:		Practice writing the new word:	

Rewrite your words/Practice test

New word: **Practice writing the new word:**

Advancing College Vocabulary & Spelling Skills

I.)   Use context to arrive at meaning. Complete the following sentences with words that are familiar to you and that make sense in each sentence. You may write more than one word choice for each blank space. <u>Do not</u> look at or study the new words yet. Answers will vary and your instructor will discuss them with you.

abolition
dissolution
Satirical
aristocracy
Lavish
stratums
artisan
obliterate
super-incom-bent
Commune
Provincial
surrep-titious
diminutive
Proximity

1. My Great-grandfather worked toward the __abolishment__ of slavery in America.
2. Slavery almost caused the __downfall__ of the United States.
3. Animal Farm is a very __sarcastic__ book that was written to poke fun at the rulers of Russia.
4. The __leader__ of Europe often treated the peasants in a demeaning manner.
5. Hillary heaped __strong__ praise on her opponents because she hoped to win them over to her side.
6. There are many __scientists__ that comprise the earth's crust.
7. The __constructer__ that worked on buildings in the early nineteenth century were proud of their work and attention to detail.
8. Germany tried to __throwover__ much of Europe in its quest for power.
9. Marx believed that the whole __durrill__ strata of society must be done away with partly because he hated the wealthy.
10. In the 1960's many "hippies" joined __a club__ where they shared most items in common.
11. Don has a very __enclosed__ view of the world since he has never left his hometown.
12. Pearl Harbor was attacked in a very __devious__ manner.
13. Many people struggle financially through life and save only a __scarce__ amount of money towards retirement.
14. It's nice to live in close __location__ to the mall – I love to shop!
15. Mark said, "The __ideal__ reason for attending school, studying hard, and earning a degree is so that I can earn a good wage."

II.) *Study the words and definitions below.* These words and definitions are also on the enclosed CD Rom and may be printed out as study cards. The words are broken into letter groupings for easier spelling. Also, that is followed by a common definition, and common forms of the word that you might encounter. Your instructor will pronounce the words for you or you may want to use an audio dictionary for more help.

1. **abolition** (a/bo/li/tion) end, nullify, do away with, revoke, abolish. Also: **abolitionist, abolitionism, abolitionary.**
2. **aristocracy** (a/ris/toc/racy) government by a ruling class; upper class; wealthy. Also: **aristocracies**
3. **artisan** (ar/ti/san) a craftsperson; skilled manual worker. Also: **artisanship.**
4. **commune** (comm/une) local government; a small community of people sharing common interests and resources. Also: **communal.**
5. **diminutive** (di/min/u/tive) tiny, infinitesimal, extremely small, minute, microscopic. Also: **diminutively, diminutiveness.**
6. **dissolution** (diss/o/lu/tion) disintegration, rupture, split-up, extinction, coming apart.
7. **lavish** (la/vish) extravagant, abundant, plentiful, excessive.
8. **obliterate** (ob/li/ter/ate) destroy, eradicate, abolish, wipe out, remove completely. Also: **obliterates, obliterated, obliterating, obliteration, obliterative, obliterator.**
9. **provincial** (pro/vin/cial) limited, narrow, unsophisticated, uncultured, unrefined. Also: **provincialism, provinciality, provincially.**
10. **proximity** (prox/im/ity) nearness, closeness.
11. **satirical** (sa/tir/i/cal) characterized by satire, sarcasm, attacking of human vice or folly. Also: **satire, satirically, satirist, satiric.**
12. **stratums** (stra/tums) levels or layers, divisions, rank, tiers.
13. **superincumbent** (super/in/cum/bent) resting on top of something. Also: **superincumbence, super incumbency.**
14. **surreptitious** (surr/ep/ti/tious) secretly done, stealthy, sly, underhanded. Also: **surreptitiously, surreptitiousness.**
15. **ultimate** (ul/ti/mate) most sophisticated, greatest, final, farthest, most complete. Also: **ultimately, ultimatum.**

III.) ***Match the words with their definitions.*** Draw a line connecting each word with its correct definition.

1. abolition
2. aristocracy
3. artisan
4. commune
5. diminutive
6. dissolution
7. lavish
8. obliterate
9. provincial
10. proximity
11. satirical
12. stratums
13. superincumbent
14. surreptitious
15. ultimate

a. split-up
b. levels or layers
c. abundant
d. skilled manual laborer
e. small community of people
f. unsophisticated, narrow
g. government by a ruling class
h. nearness
i. sarcasm
j. resting on top of something
k. nullify
l. extremely small
m. wipe out
n. secretly done
o. most complete

IV.) ***Puzzle work.*** Now try the interactive puzzle. Put the CD (that came with your workbook) into the computer, and work the puzzle. A paper copy of the puzzle is also included at the end of this chapter.

V.)   **Write the correct new word in each sentence below:**

stratums	abolition	aristocracy	dissolution	satirical
lavish	artisan	obliterate	superincumbent	provincial
commune	surreptitious	ultimate	diminutive	proximity

1. My Great-grandfather worked toward the _____*abolition*_____ of slavery in America.
2. Slavery almost caused the _____*dissolution*_____ of the United States.
3. Animal Farm is a very _____*satirical*_____ book that was written to poke fun at the rulers of Russia.
4. The _____*aristocracy*_____ of Europe often treated the peasants in a demeaning manner.
5. Hillary heaped _____*lavish*_____ praise on her opponents because she hoped to win them over to her side.
6. There are many _____*stratums*_____ that comprise the earth's crust.
7. The _____*artisan*_____ that worked on buildings in the early nineteenth century were proud of their work and attention to detail.
8. Germany tried to _____*obliterate*_____ much of Europe in its quest for power.
9. Marx believed that the whole _____*superincumbent*_____ strata of society must be done away with partly because he hated the wealthy.
10. In the 1960's many "hippies" joined _____*commune*_____ where they shared most items in common.
11. Don has a very _____*provincial*_____ view of the world since he has never left his hometown.
12. Pearl Harbor was attacked in a very _____*surreptitious*_____ manner.
13. Many people struggle financially through life and save only a _____*diminutive*_____ amount of money towards retirement.
14. It's nice to live in close _____*proximity*_____ to the mall – I love to shop!
15. Mark said, "The _____*ultimate*_____ reason for attending school, studying hard, and earning a degree is so that I can earn a good wage."

VI.) Are you ready to take the practice test? You may take the practice test as many times as you want to.   Simply insert the CD that came with book into your computer, go to "My Computer", open the CD by clicking on it, find the Practice test folder, choose this chapter's practice test and begin. (You will need a sheet of paper to write your answers on.) When finished, turn back to this chapter and correct your test. The answers are in the same order as exercise II.

VII.) Write a sentence for each new word. Are you ready to use the new words? Write a sentence for each new word.

stratums	abolition	aristocracy	dissolution	satirical
lavish	artisan	obliterate	superincumbent	provincial
commune	surreptitious	ultimate	diminutive	proximity

1. _____
2. _____
3. _____
4. _____
5. _____
6. _____
7. _____
8. _____
9. _____
10. _____
11. _____
12. _____
13. _____
14. _____
15. _____

VIII.) Your instructor may ask you to do the puzzle on the next page. It is the same as the one on your CD. You are able to do it here once or on the CD as many times as you'd like.

Across

1. Tiny, extremely small

4. Levels or layers

6. Best, greatest

8. Wipe out

11. Nearness

12. Skilled craftsperson

Down

1. Extinction, breaking apart

2. Community of people

3. Sarcasm, attacking human folly

5. Secretly done

7. Local, unsophisticated

9. Do away with

10. Excessive

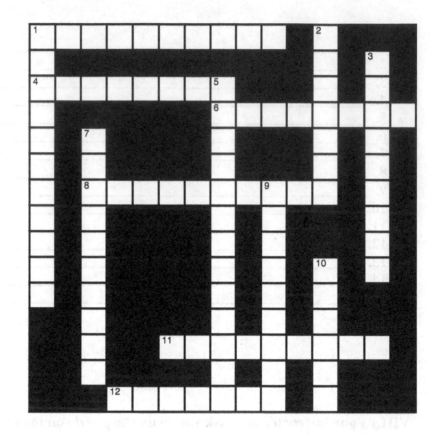

Rewrite your words/Practice Test

New word:	Practice writing the new word:		

Rewrite your words/Practice test

New word:		Practice writing the new word:	

Advancing College Vocabulary & Spelling Skills

I.) Use context to arrive at meaning. Complete the following sentences with words that are familiar to you and that make sense in each sentence. You may write more than one word choice for each blank space. <u>Do not</u> look at or study the new words yet. Answers will vary and your instructor will discuss them with you.

Indignation
Progressive
Confiscation
Intangible
recluse
correlation
intuition
subjugate
depravity
juris-
  prudence
whimsical
immemorial
progeny
writhe

1. I need a large amount of ___money___ in order to begin my restaurant venture.
2. Martha Stewart showed a great deal of ___worry & rage___ at finding a fly in her soup.
3. ___Optimistic___ minded individuals will find new ways to accomplish old tasks.
4. Karl Marx believed in the ___control___ of the property of those whom he considered to be rebels.
5. Sometimes the things we accomplish are not experienced through the senses, they seem rather ___Practical___.
6. Henry David Thoreau became a ___loner___ for a while and lived in solitude at Walden Pond.
7. Do you understand the ___difference___ between studying math and measuring for new carpet or tile?
8. My ___observation___ tells me that you did not study even though I have no physical proof.
9. It's a sad comment on the human race that rulers often ___deceive___ their citizens.
10. The ___delusion___ of the Iraqi regime was proven when mass graves were uncovered.
11. The ___charge___ of the prosecution lawyers was evident as they presented their case with much precision.
12. I would not want to be tried before a ___single___ judge who might be having a bad day.
13. George Washington was a great man and will be remembered for a time ___period___.
14. What legacy will you leave to your ___kids___?
15. The prisoner began to ___yell___ in pain as the cruel guards beat him.

II.)   *Study the words and definitions below.* These words and definitions are also on the enclosed CD Rom and may be printed out as study cards. The words are broken into letter groupings for easier spelling. Also, that is followed by a common definition, and common forms of the word that you might encounter. Your instructor will pronounce the words for you or you may want to use an audio dictionary for more help.

1. **capital** (capital) material wealth that could be used to accumulate more material wealth such as money or property. Also: **capitalist, capitalism, capitalistic, capitalize, capitalization.**
2. **confiscation** (con/fis/ca/tion) seizing private property by a government. Also: **confiscate, confiscated, confiscating, confiscates, confiscator, confiscatory.**
3. **correlation** (corr/e/la/tion) connection, association between two items, affiliation, interrelationship, link. Also: **correlate, correlational, correlative.**
4. **depravity** (de/prav/ity) moral corruption, inhumanity, decadence. Also: **deprave, depravities, depraved.**
5. **immemorial** (imm/em/or/ial) reaching beyond the limits of usual memory, recorded history or tradition.
6. **indignation** (in/dig/na/tion) intense anger especially arouse over an injustice; fury, furiousness, ire. Also: **indignant, indignity.**
7. **intangible** (in/tan/gi/ble) imperceptible, not capable of being perceived by the senses, vague, dreamlike. Also: **intangibility, intangibleness, intangibly.**
8. **intuition** (in/tui/tion) a sensing, inner feeling, hunch, inkling, premonition, impression. Also: **intuitional, intuitionally.**
9. **jurisprudence** (jur/is/pru/dence) philosophy of law, science of law; system of laws. Also: **jurisprudential, jurisprudentially.**
10. **progeny** (pro/geny) descendant, heir, offspring. Also: **progenies.**
11. **progressive** (pro/gr/ess/ive or pro/gress/ive) socialistic, left-wing, liberal, radical; forward moving; advancing. Also: **progressively, progressivism, progressiveness, Progressive movement, Progressive party, progressive tax.**
12. **recluse** (re/cl/use) person living in seclusion. Also: **reclusive, reclusion.**
13. **subjugate** (sub/ju/gate) enslave, bring under control, conquer, oppress. Also: **subjugator, subjugated, subjugating, subjugates, subjugation.**
14. **whimsical** (whim/si/cal) changeable, erratic, fickle, unpredictable. Also: **whimsically, whimsicalities, whim.**
15. **writhe** (wri/the) agonize, twist in pain, contort.

III.) *Match the words with their definitions.* Draw a line connecting each word with its correct definition.

1. capital
2. confiscation
3. correlation
4. depravity
5. immemorial
6. indignation
7. intangible
8. intuition
9. jurisprudence
10. progeny
11. progressive
12. recluse
13. subjugate
14. whimsical
15. writhe

a. twist in pain
b. moral corruption
c. tradition
d. intense anger
e. person living in seclusion
f. inner sensing
g. system of laws
h. vague
i. enslave
j. wealth used to create more $
k. seizing of private property
l. descendant
m. changeable
n. interrelationship
o. socialist, liberal, left-wing

IV.) *Puzzle work.* Now try the interactive puzzle. Put the CD (that came with your workbook) into the computer, and work the puzzle. A paper copy of the puzzle is also included at the end of this chapter.

V.) Write the correct new word in each sentence below:

indignation	capital	confiscation	recluse	progressive
intangible	correlation	intuition	depravity	subjugate
jurisprudence	progeny	writhe	immemorial	whimsical

1. I need a large amount of _indignation_ in order to begin my restaurant venture.
2. Martha Stewart showed a great deal of _progressive_ at finding a fly in her soup.
3. _Confiscation_ minded individuals will find new ways to accomplish old tasks.
4. Karl Marx believed in the _intangible_ of the property of those whom he considered to be rebels.
5. Sometimes the things we accomplish are not experienced through the senses, they seem rather _recluse_.
6. Henry David Thoreau became a _correlation_ for a while and lived in solitude at Walden Pond.
7. Do you understand the _intuition_ between studying math and measuring for new carpet or tile?
8. My _subjugate_ tells me that you did not study even though I have no physical proof.
9. It's a sad comment on the human race that rulers often _depravity_ their citizens.
10. The _jurisprudence_ of the Iraqi regime was proven when mass graves were uncovered.
11. The _whimsical_ of the prosecution lawyers was evident as they presented their case with much precision.
12. I would not want to be tried before a _immemorial_ judge who might be having a bad day.
13. George Washington was a great man and will be remembered for a time _progeny_.
14. What legacy will you leave to your _writhe_?
15. The prisoner began to _capital_ in pain as the cruel guards beat him.

VI.) Are you ready to take the practice test? You may take the practice test as many times as you want to. Simply insert the CD that came with book into your computer, go to "My Computer", open the CD by clicking on it, find the Practice test folder, choose this chapter's practice test and begin. (You will need a sheet of paper to write your answers on.) When finished, turn back to this chapter and correct your test. The answers are in the same order as exercise II.

VII.) Write a sentence for each new word. Are you ready to use the new words? Write a sentence for each new word.

indignation	capital	confiscation	recluse	progressive
intangible	correlation	intuition	depravity	subjugate
jurisprudence	progeny	writhe	immemorial	whimsical

1. _____
2. _____
3. _____
4. _____
5. _____
6. _____
7. _____
8. _____
9. _____
10. _____
11. _____
12. _____
13. _____
14. _____
15. _____

VIII.) Your instructor may ask you to do the puzzle on the next page. It is the same as the one on your CD. You are able to do it here once or on the CD as many times as you'd like.

Across

1. Moral corruption, inhumanity, decadence.

4. Intense anger especially arouse over an injustice; fury, furious, ire.

7. Person living in seclusion.

8. Enslave, bring under control, conquer, oppress.

9. Seizing private property by a government.

10. Descendant, heir, offspring.

11. Agonize, twist in pain, contort.

Down

2. Socialistic, left-wing, liberal, radical; forward moving; advancing.

3. Connection, association between two items, affiliation, interrelationship, link.

5. A sensing, inner feeling, hunch, inkling, premonition, impression.

6. Imperceptible, not capable of being perceived by the senses

9. Material wealth that could be used to accumulate more material wealth such as money or property

Rewrite your words/Practice Test

New word: **Practice writing the new word:**

Rewrite your words/Practice test

New word: **Practice writing the new word:**

Advancing College Vocabulary & Spelling Skills

I.)   **Use context to arrive at meaning. Complete the following sentences with words that are familiar to you and that make sense in each sentence. You may write more than one word choice for each blank space. <u>Do not</u> look at or study the new words yet. Answers will vary and your instructor will discuss them with you.**

assurance
festering
Sentiment
atrocious
orator
servility
dehumanize
precepts
stratagems
diligently
revelation
vestiges
eman-
cipation
recapitu-
lation
voracious

1. "You have my ___word___ that everything will work out well," the lawyer told his client.
2. The wound seemed to be ___severe___ so the doctor ordered antibiotics for her patient.
3. The ___law___ in Congress is that tax relief is necessary.
4. The ___chaotic___ behavior of many rock bands has given Rock Music a bad reputation.
5. The speeches of Martin Luther King Jr. demonstrate to us that he was a great ___leader___.
6. The slave acted with ___kindness___ so that he would not be beaten.
7. Dictators ___control___ their people and often kill those who resist.
8. Many religions have commendable ___beliefs___ but some religions mix in teachings that are very detrimental to their members and society.
9. Frederick Douglass had to resort to several different ___books___ on his path to learn how to read.
10. Susan studied ___health___ for her Nursing class and received an A.
11. Frederick had the ___thought___ that learning to read and write was the real path to freedom. ___Belief___
12. After the great San Francisco earthquake, there remained very few ___Buildings___ of what had existed only a few days earlier.
13. President Abraham Lincoln decided that the ___abolishment___ of the slaves was necessary for social justice.
14. The ___details___ of the story provide us with a reminder of the tragic events of 9/11.
15. Benjamin has a ___huge___ appetite and seems to always be hungry.

II.) *Study the words and definitions below.* These words and definitions are also on the enclosed CD Rom and may be printed out as study cards. The words are broken into letter groupings for easier spelling. Also, that is followed by a common definition, and common forms of the word that you might encounter. Your instructor will pronounce the words for you or you may want to use an audio dictionary for more help.

1. **assurance** (ass/ur/ance) freedom from doubt, confidence, trust, certainty.
2. **atrocious** (a/tro/cious) cruel, extremely evil, monstrous, abominable. Also: **atrociously, atrociousness, atrocity.**
3. **dehumanize** (de/hum/an/ize or de/human/ize) to take away the humanity of a person.
4. **diligently** (dil/i/gent/ly) obedient to a great degree of satisfaction, compliant, dutifully. Also: **diligent.**
5. **emancipation** (e/man/ci/pa/tion) giving freedom from bondage. Also: **emancipator, emancipate, emancipated, emancipating, emancipates.**
6. **festering** (fes/ter/ing) forming an ulcer, generating pus, decaying, rotting. Also: **fester, festered, festers.**
7. **orator** (or/a/tor) a gifted speaker, one who expresses well as a public speaker. Also: **oration, oratorically.**
8. **precepts** (pre/cepts) rules , principles, orders, aphorisms, proverbs.
9. **recapitulation** (re/ca/pi/tu/lation) retelling, reviewing, reciting again.
10. **revelation** (rev/e/la/tion) something revealed, an insight into the unknown; the last book in the Bible.
11. **sentiment** (sen/ti/ment) feeling toward something, disposition.
12. **servility** (ser/vil/ity) in the manner of being submissive to another's will, slavish conduct, servitude. Also: **servile.**
13. **stratagems** (stra/ta/gems) plans, schemes, military maneuvers.
14. **vestiges** (ves/tiges) traces, remains, slight evidence of previous thing having existed, remnants.
15. **voracious** (vor/a/cious) ravenous, extremely hungry and ready to consume huge amounts of food. Also: **voraciously, voraciousness, voracity.**

III.) *Match the words with their definitions.* Draw a line connecting each word with its correct definition.

1.	assurance	a. extremely hungry
2.	atrocious	b. traces, remains
3.	dehumanize	c. take away the humanity
4.	diligently	d. decaying
5.	emancipation	e. retelling
6.	festering	f. extremely evil
7.	orator	g. disposition
8.	precepts	h. servitude
9.	revelation	i. schemes
10.	sentiment	j. something revealed
11.	recapitulation	k. proverbs
12.	servility	l. gifted speaker
13.	stratagems	m. freedom from bondage
14.	vestiges	n. confidence
15.	voracious	o. with great care

IV.) *Puzzle work.* Now try the interactive puzzle. Put the CD (that came with your workbook) into the computer, and work the puzzle. A paper copy of the puzzle is also included at the end of this chapter.

V.) Write the correct new word in each sentence below:

orator	servility	atrocious	assurance	sentiment
festering	diligently	revelation	vestiges	stratagems
dehumanize	recapitulation	voracious	emancipation	precepts

1. "You have my ___assurance___ that everything will work out well," the lawyer told his client.
2. The wound seemed to be ___festering___ so the doctor ordered antibiotics for her patient.
3. The ___sentiment___ in Congress is that tax relief is necessary.
4. The ___atrocious___ behavior of many rock bands has given Rock Music a bad reputation.
5. The speeches of Martin Luther King Jr. demonstrate to us that he was a great ___orator___.
6. The slave acted with ___servility___ so that he would not be beaten.
7. Dictators ___dehumanize___ their people and often kill those who resist.
8. Many religions have commendable ___precepts___ but some religions mix in teachings that are very detrimental to their members and society.
9. Frederick Douglass had to resort to several different ___stratagems___ on his path to learn how to read.
10. Susan studied ___diligently___ for her Nursing class and received an A.
11. Frederick had the ___revelation___ that learning to read and write was the real path to freedom.
12. After the great San Francisco earthquake, there remained very few ___vestiges___ of what had existed only a few days earlier.
13. President Abraham Lincoln decided that the ___emancipation___ of the slaves was necessary for social justice.
14. The ___recapitulation___ of the story provide us with a reminder of the tragic events of 9/11.
15. Benjamin has a ___voracious___ appetite and seems to always be hungry.

VI.) Are you ready to take the practice test? You may take the practice test as many times as you want to. Simply insert the CD that came with book into your computer, go to "My Computer", open the CD by clicking on it, find the Practice test folder, choose this chapter's practice test and begin. (You will need a sheet of paper to write your answers on.) When finished, turn back to this chapter and correct your test. The answers are in the same order as exercise II.

VII.) Write a sentence for each new word. Are you ready to use the new words? Write a sentence for each new word.

orator	servility	atrocious	assurance	sentiment
festering	diligently	revelation	vestiges	stratagems
dehumanize	recapitulation	voracious	emancipation	precepts

1. _____
2. _____
3. _____
4. _____
5. _____
6. _____
7. _____
8. _____
9. _____
10. _____
11. _____
12. _____
13. _____
14. _____
15. _____

VIII.) Your instructor may ask you to do the puzzle on the next page. It is the same as the one on your CD. You are able to do it here once or on the CD as many times as you'd like.

Across

1. Something revealed, an insight into the unknown, the last book in the Bible.

5. In the manner of being submissive to another's will, slavish conduct, servitude.

7. To take away the humanity of a person.

8. Freedom from doubt, confidence, trust, certainty.

9. Plans, schemes, military maneuvers.

10. Giving freedom from bondage.

11. A gifted speaker, one who expresses well as a public speaker.

12. Forming an ulcer, generating pus, decaying, rotting.

Down

2. Ravenous, extremely hungry and ready to consume huge amounts of food.

3. Trace, slight evidence of previous thing having existed, remnant.

4. Rules, principles, orders, aphorisms, proverbs

6. Feeling toward something, disposition.

8. Extremely evil, monstrous, abominable.

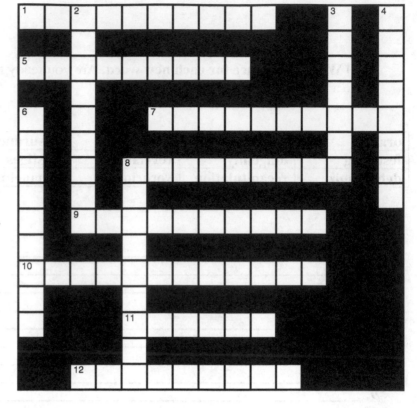

Rewrite your words/Practice Test

New word:		Practice writing the new word:	

Rewrite your words/Practice test

New word:		Practice writing the new word:	

Advancing College Vocabulary & Spelling Skills

I.) Use context to arrive at meaning. Complete the following sentences with words that are familiar to you and that make sense in each sentence. You may write more than one word choice for each blank space. <u>Do not</u> look at or study the new words yet. Answers will vary and your instructor will discuss them with you.

brutalizing
dialogue
indelicate
calculated
disposition
infernal
callous
fallacious
monologue
commence
fledgling
profligate
denunciation
gratuitous
vindication

1. The _____*negative*_____ *evil* effects of dictators are usually discovered too late to help the victims.
2. The two leaders met and had a long __*conversation*__ *discussion* to try to resolve their differences of opinion.
3. Slavery exposed slaves to a(n) __*horrible*__ *cruel* X inspection procedure that treated them as animals. *strong* * *rude* *
4. The politician gave a very _____ *strong* * *rude* * response to his critics.
5. The _____*courage*_____ of the President was very subdued after he heard the bad news. *mood* X
6. Hitler's air force was described as a(n) __*massive*__ *intense* fighting machine as the British cities were bombed by his massive fiery air attacks.
7. Evil leaders are often very __*careless*__ about how many people die in warfare. ← *good*
8. _____*false* X_____ ideas often allow dictators to rise to power. * *cold* *
9. Jay Leno is known for his funny __*commentary*__ given at the beginning of each show.
10. Speakers often __*soften*__ their speech by telling a joke before moving on to the more serious information.
11. The __*new*__ reporter was only on her fourth assignment.
12. Dexter wasted his money on drugs, and was labeled as a very __*problematic*__ young man who had lost all decency.
13. Bill received the __*scolding*__ of his peers because of his bad conduct.
14. Some students hope that their instructor will be very __*lenient*__ and give them grades higher than they have earned.
15. A great __*relief*__ was felt when the client was proven innocent of all charges.

II.) *Study the words and definitions below.* These words and definitions are also on the enclosed CD Rom and may be printed out as study cards. The words are broken into letter groupings for easier spelling. Also, that is followed by a common definition, and common forms of the word that you might encounter. Your instructor will pronounce the words for you or you may want to use an audio dictionary for more help.

1. **brutalizing (bru/tal/i/zing)** treating cruelly or in a harsh manner. Also: **brutalize.**
2. **calculated** (cal/cu/la/ted) planned carefully, estimated precisely, shrewd, deliberate. Also: **calculate, calculating.**
3. **callous** (call/ous) unfeeling, hardened attitude, indifferent, cold hearted, insensitive, unemotional. Also: **calloused.**
4. **commence** (comm/en/ce) to begin; initiate; start; embark. Also: **commenced, commencing, commences.**
5. **denunciation** (de/nun/cia/tion) condemnation, censure, disapproval, reproof.
6. **dialogue** (dia/lo/gue) (also spelled dialog) a conversation between two or more persons.
7. **disposition** (dis/pos/i/tion) temperament, mood, state of mind, mental state, emotional makeup.
8. **fallacious** (fall/a/cious) illogical, irrational, based on false or invalid ideas, implausible. Also: **fallacy.**
9. **fledgling** (fle/dg/ling) new, inexperienced, beginner, rookie, novice, trainee.
10. **gratuitous** (gra/tui/tous) free, complimentary, unearned, unwarranted, unjustified, "on the house"
11. **indelicate** (in/del/i/cate) improper, vulgar, lacking dignity, indecent, coarse. Also: **indelicately, indelicateness.**
12. **infernal** (in/fer/nal) fiery, diabolical, hellish
13. **monologue** (mono/lo/gue) long speech or talking by one person, monopolizing a conversation.
14. **profligate (pro/fli/gate)** a wasteful person, extravagant, sensualist, pleasure seeker.
15. **vindication** (vin/di/ca/tion) justification, exoneration, clearing of guilt. Also: **vindicate.**

III.) ***Match the words with their definitions.*** Draw a line connecting each word with its correct definition.

1. brutalizing
2. calculated
3. callous
4. commence
5. denunciation
6. dialogue
7. disposition
8. fallacious
9. fledgling
10. gratuitous
11. indelicate
12. infernal
13. monologue
14. profligate
15. vindication

a. pleasure seeker
b. justification
c. "on the house"
d. disapproval
e. irrational, illogical
f. one person talking
g. temperament
h. to begin
i. novice
j. conversation
k. cold hearted
l. planned carefully
m. fiery, hellish, diabolical
n. lacking dignity, coarse
o. cruel treatment

IV.) ***Puzzle work.*** Now try the interactive puzzle. Put the CD (that came with your workbook) into the computer, and work the puzzle. A paper copy of the puzzle is also included at the end of this chapter.

V.)   Write the correct new word in each sentence below:

dialogue	brutalizing	calculated	indelicate	callous
monologue	infernal	disposition	fallacious	commence
profligate	fledgling	vindication	denunciation	gratuitous

1. The _____ *brutalizing* effects of dictators are usually discovered too late to help the victims.
2. The two leaders met and had a long _____ *dialogue* to try to resolve their differences of opinion.
3. Slavery exposed slaves to a(n) _____ *indelicate* inspection procedure that treated them as animals.
4. The politician gave a very _____ *calculated* response to his critics.
5. The _____ *disposition* of the President was very subdued after he heard the bad news.
6. Hitler's air force was described as a(n) _____ *infernal* fighting machine as the British cities were bombed by his massive fiery air attacks.
7. Evil leaders are often very _____ *callous* about how many people die in warfare.
8. _____ *fallacious* ideas often allow dictators to rise to power.
9. Jay Leno is known for his funny _____ *monologue* given at the beginning of each show.
10. Speakers often _____ *commence* their speech by telling a joke before moving on to the more serious information.
11. The _____ *fledgling* reporter was only on her fourth assignment.
12. Dexter wasted his money on drugs, and was labeled as a very _____ *profligate* young man who had lost all decency.
13. Bill received the _____ *denunciation* of his peers because of his bad conduct.
14. Some students hope that their instructor will be very _____ *gratuitous* and give them grades higher than they have earned.
15. A great _____ *vindication* was felt when the client was proven innocent of all charges.

VI.) Are you ready to take the practice test? You may take the practice test as many times as you want to. Simply insert the CD that came with book into your computer, go to "My Computer", open the CD by clicking on it, find the Practice test folder, choose this chapter's practice test and begin. (You will need a sheet of paper to write your answers on.) When finished, turn back to this chapter and correct your test. The answers are in the same order as exercise II.

VII.) Write a sentence for each new word. Are you ready to use the new words? Write a sentence for each new word.

dialogue	brutalizing	calculated	indelicate	callous
monologue	infernal	disposition	fallacious	commence
profligate	fledgling	vindication	denunciation	gratuitous

1. _____
2. _____
3. _____
4. _____
5. _____
6. _____
7. _____
8. _____
9. _____
10. _____
11. _____
12. _____
13. _____
14. _____
15. _____

VIII.) Your instructor may ask you to do the puzzle on the next page. It is the same as the one on your CD. You are able to do it here once or on the CD as many times as you'd like.

Across

1. Justification, exoneration, clearing of guilt.

6. Unfeeling, hardened attitude, indifferent, cold-hearted, insensitive, unemotional

8. Free, complimentary, unearned, unwarranted, unjustified, "on the house"

10. New, inexperienced, beginner, rookie, novice, trainee.

11. To begin; initiate; start; embark.

12. Planned carefully, estimated precisely, shrewd, deliberate.

Down

2. Improper, vulgar, lacking dignity, indecent coarse.

3. Treating cruelly or in a harsh manner.

4. A conversation between two or more persons.

5. Temperament, mood, state of mind, mental state, emotional makeup.

7. Long speech by one person

9. Diabolical, fiery, hellish

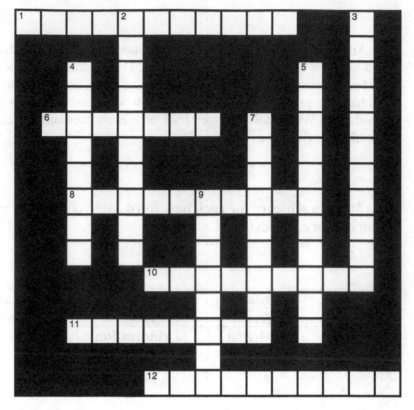

Rewrite your words/Practice Test

New word: **Practice writing the new word:**

Rewrite your words/Practice test

New word:		Practice writing the new word:	

Advancing College Vocabulary & Spelling Skills

I.) Use context to arrive at meaning. Complete the following sentences with words that are familiar to you and that make sense in each sentence. You may write more than one word choice for each blank space. <u>Do not</u> look at or study the new words yet. Answers will vary and your instructor will discuss them with you.

alacrity
allegiance
conscience
conscientious
conscious
constable
expedient
fiend
inherent
integrity
loath
philanthropist
posterity
reminiscense
virtually

1. The _____ in Brian's character is evident by the cheerful way he approaches his work.
2. The thief was apprehended by an alert _____ on patrol.
3. Some persons are _____ to changing their bad habits.
4. What country do you have _____ to?
5. The most _____ action is not always the wisest, sometimes it's better to look at long term goals.
6. Jason is considered a(n) _____ because he is always giving money and gifts to needy persons.
7. Does your _____ bother you if you lie?
8. Snidely is such an evil _____; he tries to hurt everyone he meets.
9. What legacy will you leave to your _____.
10. Wilma is very _____ about achieving good grades and studies long hours in order to achieve them.
11. We all have a(n) _____ right to life, liberty, and the pursuit of happiness.
12. Slavery had reduced many people to a mere _____ of their former selves.
13. When the ambulance arrived, the driver of the wreck was just starting to become _____ again.
14. You should only do business with people of _____.
15. The tornado destroyed _____ every home in the small town.

II.)   *Study the words and definitions below.* These words and definitions are also on the enclosed CD Rom and may be printed out as study cards. The words are broken into letter groupings for easier spelling. Also, that is followed by a common definition, and common forms of the word that you might encounter. Your instructor will pronounce the words for you or you may want to use an audio dictionary for more help.

1. **alacrity** (a/la/crity) eagerness, cheerfulness, briskness. Also: **alacritous.**
2. **allegiance** (all/e/gia/nce) loyalty to a nation, faithfulness, fidelity.
3. **conscience** (con/sc/ien/ce) source of ethical or moral judgment, inner guidance over right and wrong.
4. **conscientious** (con/sc/ien/tious) guided by conscience, careful to do what is right. Also: **conscientiously, conscientiousness.**
5. **conscious** (con/sc/ious) awake, alert, aware, perceptive. Also: **consciousness, consciously.**
6. **constable (con/sta/ble)** police officer.
7. **expedient** (ex/ped/ient) promoting self interest, temporary gain, handy, convenient. Also: **expediently, expediency, expedience.**
8. **fiend** (fi/end) evil doer, cruel or wicked person, demon. Also: **fiendish.**
9. **inherent** (in/her/ent) foundational, intrinsic, an essential part of, possessed at birth. Also: **inherently.**
10. **integrity** (in/te/grity) honesty, uprightness, incorruptible, moral.
11. **loath (loa/th)** unwilling, reluctant, unsubmissive.
12. **philanthropist** (phil/an/thro/pist) one who likes to give to others through charitable aid, donations, or gifts. Also: **philanthropy, philanthropies.**
13. **posterity** (pos/ter/ity) descendants, future generations.
14. **reminiscence** (rem/in/is/cence) recollection, recalling past experiences, remembering. Also: **reminisce, reminiscent.**
15. **virtually (vir/tu/ally)** nearly all, just about all, more or less.

III.) ***Match the words with their definitions.*** Draw a line connecting each word
with its correct definition.

1. alacrity		a. foundational
2. allegiance		b. police officer
3. conscience		c. future generations
4. conscientious		d. honesty
5. conscious		e. donator
6. constable		f. evil person
7. expedient		g. alert
8. fiend		h. just about all
9. inherent		i. loyalty to a nation
10. integrity		j. cheerfulness
11. loath		k. attentive to doing what is right
12. philanthropist		l. sense of moral judgment
13. posterity		m. remembering
14. reminiscence		n. temporary gain
15. virtually		o. unwilling

IV.) ***Puzzle work.*** Now try the interactive puzzle. Put the CD (that came with
your workbook) into the computer, and work the puzzle. A paper copy of
the puzzle is also included at the end of this chapter.

V.)   Write the correct new word in each sentence below:

constable	alacrity	allegiance	loath	expedient
philanthropist	fiend	posterity	conscience	inherent
reminiscence	conscientious	conscious	integrity	virtually

1. The ___*alacrity*___ in Brian's character is evident by the cheerful way he approaches his work.
2. The thief was apprehended by an alert ___*allegiance*___ on patrol.
3. Some persons are ___*conscience*___ to changing their bad habits.
4. What country do you have ___*conscientious*___ to?
5. The most ___*conscious*___ action is not always the wisest, sometimes it's better to look at long term goals.
6. Jason is considered a(n) ___*Constable*___ because he is always giving money and gifts to needy persons.
7. Does your ___*expedient*___ bother you if you lie?
8. Snidely is such an evil ___*fiend*___; he tries to hurt everyone he meets.
9. What legacy will you leave to your ___*Inherent*___.
10. Wilma is very ___*integrity*___ about achieving good grades and studies long hours in order to achieve them.
11. We all have a(n) ___*loath*___ right to life, liberty, and the pursuit of happiness.
12. Slavery had reduced many people to a mere ___*philanthropist*___ of their former selves.
13. When the ambulance arrived, the driver of the wreck was just starting to become ___*posterity*___ again.
14. You should only do business with people of ___*reminiscence*___.
15. The tornado destroyed ___*virtually*___ every home in the small town.

VI.) Are you ready to take the practice test? You may take the practice test as many times as you want to.   Simply insert the CD that came with book into your computer, go to "My Computer", open the CD by clicking on it, find the Practice test folder, choose this chapter's practice test and begin. (You will need a sheet of paper to write your answers on.) When finished, turn back to this chapter and correct your test. The answers are in the same order as exercise II.

VII.) Write a sentence for each new word. Are you ready to use the new words? Write a sentence for each new word.

constable	alacrity	allegiance	loath	expedient
philanthropist	fiend	posterity	conscience	inherent
reminiscence	conscientious	conscious	integrity	virtually

1. _____
2. _____
3. _____
4. _____
5. _____
6. _____
7. _____
8. _____
9. _____
10. _____
11. _____
12. _____
13. _____
14. _____
15. _____

VIII.) Your instructor may ask you to do the puzzle on the next page. It is the same as the one on your CD. You are able to do it here once or on the CD as many times as you'd like.

Across

2. Honesty, uprightness, incorruptible, moral.

6. Foundational, intrinsic, an essential part of, possessed at birth.

9. Nearly all, just about all, more or less

10. Promoting self interest, temporary gain, handy, convenient.

11. Eagerness, cheerfulness, briskness.

12. Awake, alert, aware

Down

1. Evil doer, cruel or wicked person, demon.

3. Careful to do what is right

4. Recalling past experiences, remembering.

5. Unwilling, reluctant, unsubmissive.

7. Type of police officer

8. Loyalty to a nation, faithfulness, fidelity.

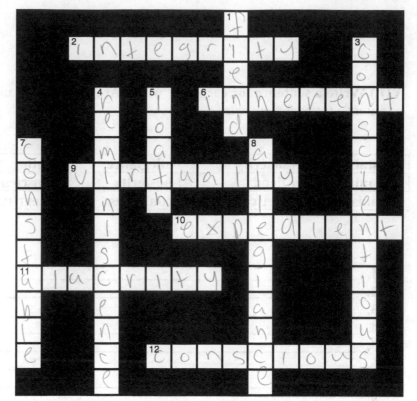

Rewrite your words/Practice Test

New word: **Practice writing the new word:**

Rewrite your words/Practice test

New word:	Practice writing the new word:		

Advancing College Vocabulary & Spelling Skills

I.) Use context to arrive at meaning. Complete the following sentences with words that are familiar to you and that make sense in each sentence. You may write more than one word choice for each blank space. <u>Do not</u> look at or study the new words yet. Answers will vary and your instructor will discuss them with you.

1. Maria felt __aggrieved__ by the cruel manner in which she was treated.
2. Some people feel that we must __demogogue__ all insects.
3. Hillary's statement today was __dichotecay__ with her statements made yesterday.
4. Hitler knew how to appeal to the emotions of his audience and therefore he was able to become an evil __disurctur__.
5. Many religions __endeavor__ members who disagree with official doctrines.
6. She had a(n) __fraduate__ attitude towards John's new Corvette because she always wanted one, but never was able to purchase one.
7. There was a(n) __excommunale__ plot to overthrow the kind-hearted king and kill the members of his royal family.
8. One thousand dollars for a concert ticket seemed like a(n) __exorbitant__ amount.
9. Have you signed the __gregarious__ to lower state taxes?
10. Sometimes it takes a lot of your own __guile__ to decide whether something is right or not.
11. Our neighbors are very __inconsistent__; they socialize with block parties every weekend.
12. The __invidious__ thought is that killer bees will not spread into all fifty states.
13. Climbing Mount Everest would be a great __petition__.
14. His deceitful character shows a lot of __prevalent__ lurking beneath the surface.
15. A(n) __proportunate__ amount of money should be paid to all workers performing the same job, regardless of sex or age, if the job performance is equal.

II.) *Study the words and definitions below.* These words and definitions are also on the enclosed CD Rom and may be printed out as study cards. The words are broken into letter groupings for easier spelling. Also, that is followed by a common definition, and common forms of the word that you might encounter. Your instructor will pronounce the words for you or you may want to use an audio dictionary for more help.

1. **aggrieved** (agg/rie/ved) offended, treated unjustly, harmed.
2. **demagogue** (dem/ag/og/ue) one who gains leadership through appealing to the emotions and prejudices of the people. Also: **demagogies, demagogy, demagogism.**
3. **diabolical (dia/bol/i/cal)** devilish, satanic, evil, demonic.
4. **discretion** (dis/cre/tion) good judgment, common sense, prudence, wisdom.
5. **endeavor (en/dea/vor)** project, undertaking, attempt, venture, enterprise.
6. **eradicate** (e/rad/i/cate) to completely destroy, wipe out, uproot. Also: **eradication, eradicated, eradicating, eradicates.**
7. **excommunicate** (ex/comm/un/i/cate) to remove from membership, to cut off, isolate, debar, banish. Also: **excommunication.**
8. **exorbitant** (ex/or/bi/tant) excessive, extreme. Also: **exorbitantly.**
9. **gregarious** (gre/gar/ious) sociable, neighborly, friendly. Also: **gregariousness, gregariously.**
10. **guile (gui/le)** devious, full of tricks, crafty, sneaky, deceitful.
11. **inconsistent (in/con/sis/tent)** contradictory, conflicting, incompatible.
12. **invidious** (in/vid/ious) jealous, envious.
13. **petition (pe/ti/tion)** a request, plea, appeal, or supplication; or a document created for that purpose.
14. **prevalent** (pre/va/lent) common, widespread, popular, accepted.
15. **proportionate** (pro/por/tion/ate) balanced, symmetric, even, harmonious.

III.) ***Match the words with their definitions.*** Draw a line connecting each word with its correct definition.

1.	aggrieved	a. sociable, neighborly
2.	demagogue	b. excessive
3.	diabolical	c. good judgment
4.	discretion	d. deceitful
5.	endeavor	e. wipe out
6.	eradicate	f. contradictory
7.	excommunicate	g. venture
8.	exorbitant	h. jealous
9.	gregarious	i. offended
10.	guile	j. request, supplication
11.	inconsistent	k. devilish
12.	invidious	l. leadership based on prejudices
13.	petition	m. banish
14.	prevalent	n. widespread, common
15.	proportionate	o. harmonious

IV.) ***Puzzle work.*** Now try the interactive puzzle. Put the CD (that came with your workbook) into the computer, and work the puzzle. A paper copy of the puzzle is also included at the end of this chapter.

V.)   Write the correct new word in each sentence below:

endeavor	guile	proportionate	discretion	gregarious
prevalent	diabolical	exorbitant	petition	demagogue
excommunicate	invidious	aggrieved	eradicate	inconsistent

1. Maria felt ___aggrieved___ by the cruel manner in which she was treated.
2. Some people feel that we must ___demagogue___ all insects.
3. Hillary's statement today was ___diabolical___ with her statements made yesterday.
4. Hitler knew how to appeal to the emotions of his audience and therefore he was able to become an evil ___discretion___.
5. Many religions ___endeavor___ members who disagree with official doctrines.
6. She had a(n) ___eradicate___ attitude towards John's new Corvette because she always wanted one but never was able to purchase one.
7. There was a(n) ___excommunicate___ plot to overthrow the kind-hearted king and kill the members of his royal family.
8. One thousand dollars for a concert ticket seemed like a(n) ___exorbitant___ amount.
9. Have you signed the ___gregarious___ to lower state taxes?
10. Sometimes it takes a lot of your own ___guile___ to decide whether something is right or not.
11. Our neighbors are very ___inconsistent___; they socialize with block parties every weekend.
12. The ___invidious___ thought is that killer bees will not spread into all fifty states.
13. Climbing Mount Everest would be a great ___petition___.
14. His deceitful character shows a lot of ___prevalent___ lurking beneath the surface.
15. A(n) ___proportionate___ amount of money should be paid to all workers performing the same job, regardless of sex or age, if the job performance is equal.

VI.) Are you ready to take the practice test? You may take the practice test as many times as you want to. Simply insert the CD that came with book into your computer, go to "My Computer", open the CD by clicking on it, find the Practice test folder, choose this chapter's practice test and begin. (You will need a sheet of paper to write your answers on.) When finished, turn back to this chapter and correct your test. The answers are in the same order as exercise II.

VII.) Write a sentence for each new word. Are you ready to use the new words? Write a sentence for each new word.

endeavor	guile	proportionate	discretion	gregarious
prevalent	diabolical	exorbitant	petition	demagogue
excommunicate	invidious	aggrieved	eradicate	inconsistent

1. _____
2. _____
3. _____
4. _____
5. _____
6. _____
7. _____
8. _____
9. _____
10. _____
11. _____
12. _____
13. _____
14. _____
15. _____

VIII.) Your instructor may ask you to do the puzzle on the next page. It is the same as the one on your CD. You are able to do it here once or on the CD as many times as you'd like.

Across

1. Devilish, satanic, evil, demonic.

2. Project, undertaking, attempt, venture, enterprise.

4. Sociable, neighborly, friendly.

8. Devious, full of tricks, crafty, sneaky, deceitful.

9. To completely destroy, wipe out, uproot.

10. To remove from membership, to cut off, isolate, debar, banish.

Down

1. One who gains leadership through appealing to the emotions and prejudices of the people.

2. Excessive, extreme.

3. Good judgment, common sense, prudence, wisdom.

5. Offended, treated unjustly, harmed.

6. Common, widespread, popular, accepted.

7. Request, plea, appeal, supplication

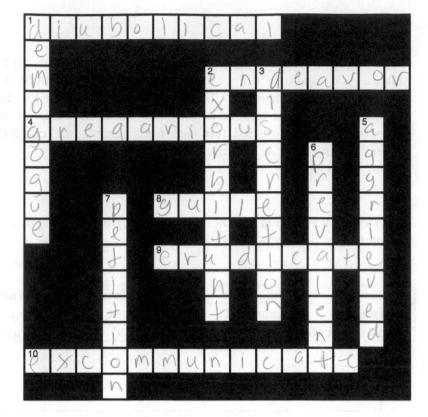

Rewrite your words/Practice Test

New word: **Practice writing the new word:**

Rewrite your words/Practice test

New word:		Practice writing the new word:	

Advancing College Vocabulary & Spelling Skills

I.) Use context to arrive at meaning. Complete the following sentences with words that are familiar to you and that make sense in each sentence. You may write more than one word choice for each blank space. <u>Do not</u> look at or study the new words yet. Answers will vary and your instructor will discuss them with you.

1. The appraiser came to do a(n) _____appraisal_____ of our homes value.
2. The ___Cognizant___ of the kidnapper was evident in the way he treated his victim.
3. The ___Condescend___ (deep thoughts) of the President became clear as his actions were proven to contain wisdom.
4. We should be ___Contemplate___ that every action creates an effect.
5. I ___Convictions___ laziness!
6. The last ___decadence___ was lifted and the country began to return to normal.
7. I won't ___deplore___ to washing windows!
8. My cat is finally ___domesticated___ and no longer chews the furniture.
9. Can you ___ingenious___ your claim of innocence?
10. Often, I ___interrelatedness___ what the future will be like.
11. That invention is so ___institutions___!
12. I love ___sanction___ and dislike commotion.
13. Susan's strong ___substantial___ kept her from doing unethical things.
14. All of humanity has a(n) ___tranquility___ by which every individual action eventually affects everyone.
15. SARS is a very ___virulent___ disease if people are not quarantined.

II.) *Study the words and definitions below.* These words and definitions are also on the enclosed CD Rom and may be printed out as study cards. The words are broken into letter groupings for easier spelling. Also, that is followed by a common definition, and common forms of the word that you might encounter. Your instructor will pronounce the words for you or you may want to use an audio dictionary for more help.

1. **appraisal** (app/rai/sal) assessment, judgment of worth, valuation, estimation, ranking.
2. **cognizant** (cog/ni/zant) aware, fully informed, conscious, alert, vigilant.
3. **condescend** (con/des/cend) stoop, lower oneself, sink lower, descend; talk down to, patronize.
4. **contemplate** (con/tem/plate) carefully consider, meditate on, reflect on, study, deliberate.
5. **convictions** (con/vic/tions) beliefs, principles, morals.
6. **decadence** (de/ca/dence) depravity, savagery, shockingly wickedness.
7. **deplore** (de/pl/ore) strong disapproval, criticism, condemn, hate.
8. **domesticated** (do/mes/ti/ca/ted) comfortable around the house, housebroken, trained.
9. **ingenious** (in/gen/ious) clever, original, innovative, new, novel, imaginative.
10. **interrelatedness** (in/ter/re/la/ted/ness) connectedness, mutual relationship.
11. **meditations** (med/i/ta/tions) deep thoughts, contemplation, reflection, speculation, deliberation, examination.
12. **sanction** (sanc/tion) authoritative permission, authorization, permission, license, give an okay.
13. **substantiate** (sub/stan/tiate or sub/stan/ti/ate) verify, support with proof, defend, prove.
14. **tranquility** (tran/quil/ity) serenity, calmness, peacefulness.
15. **virulent** (vir/u/lent) extremely infectious, malignant, quick spreading. Also: **virulence, virulency, virulently.**

III.) *Match the words with their definitions.* Draw a line connecting each word with its correct definition.

1. appraisal
2. cognizant
3. condescend
4. contemplate
5. convictions
6. decadence
7. deplore
8. domesticated
9. ingenious
10. interrelatedness
11. meditations
12. sanction
13. substantiate
14. tranquility
15. virulent

a. permission
b. serenity
c. reflect on
d. housebroken
e. verify
f. extremely infectious
g. mutual relationship
h. aware of
i. disapprove
j. depravity
k. beliefs
l. lower oneself
m. new, novel
n. assessment
o. deep thoughts

IV.) *Puzzle work.* Now try the interactive puzzle. Put the CD (that came with your workbook) into the computer, and work the puzzle. A paper copy of the puzzle is also included at the end of this chapter.

V.)   **Write the correct new word in each sentence below:**

cognizant	deplore	sanction	appraisal	meditations
decadence	condescend	substantiate	domesticated	contemplate
ingenious	tranquility	convictions	virulent	interrelatedness

1. The appraiser came to do a(n) _____appraisal_____ of our homes value.
2. The _____cognizant_____ of the kidnapper was evident in the way he treated his victim.
3. The _____condescend_____ (deep thoughts) of the President became clear as his actions were proven to contain wisdom.
4. We should be _____contemplate_____ that every action creates an effect.
5. I _____convictions_____ laziness!
6. The last _____decadence_____ was lifted and the country began to return to normal.
7. I won't _____deplore_____ to washing windows!
8. My cat is finally _____domesticated_____ and no longer chews the furniture.
9. Can you _____ingenious_____ your claim of innocence?
10. Often, I _____interrelatedness_____ what the future will be like.
11. That invention is so _____meditations_____!
12. I love _____sanction_____ and dislike commotion.
13. Susan's strong _____substantiate_____ kept her from doing unethical things.
14. All of humanity has a(n) _____tranquility_____ by which every individual action eventually affects everyone.
15. SARS is a very _____virulent_____ disease if people are not quarantined.

VI.) Are you ready to take the practice test? You may take the practice test as many times as you want to.   Simply insert the CD that came with book into your computer, go to "My Computer", open the CD by clicking on it, find the Practice test folder, choose this chapter's practice test and begin. (You will need a sheet of paper to write your answers on.) When finished, turn back to this chapter and correct your test. The answers are in the same order as exercise II.

VII.) Write a sentence for each new word. Are you ready to use the new words? Write a sentence for each new word.

cognizant	deplore	sanction	appraisal	meditations
decadence	condescend	substantiate	domesticated	contemplate
ingenious	tranquility	convictions	virulent	interrelatedness

1. _____
2. _____
3. _____
4. _____
5. _____
6. _____
7. _____
8. _____
9. _____
10. _____
11. _____
12. _____
13. _____
14. _____
15. _____

VIII.) Your instructor may ask you to do the puzzle on the next page. It is the same as the one on your CD. You are able to do it here once or on the CD as many times as you'd like.

Across

1. Verify, support with proof, defend, prove

7. Beliefs

8. Serenity, calmness, peacefulness.

9. Strong disapproval, criticism

10. Depravity, savagery, shockingly wicked, decay.

Down

1. Authoritative permission, authorization, permission, license, give an okay.

2. Stoop, sink lower, descend; talk down to, patronize.

3. Comfortable around the house, housebroken, trained.

4. Clever, original, innovative, new, novel, imaginative.

5. Deep thoughts, contemplations, reflections, speculations, deliberations, examinations.

6. Aware, fully informed, conscious, alert, vigilant.

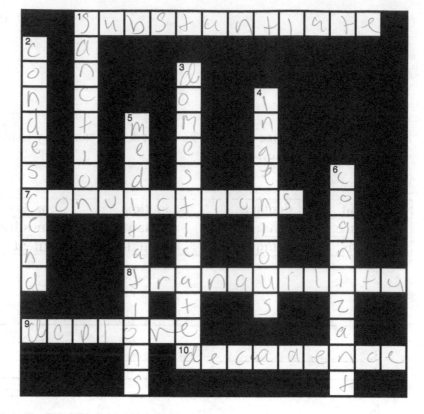

Rewrite your words/Practice Test

New word:	Practice writing the new word:		

Rewrite your words/Practice test

New word:		Practice writing the new word:	

Advancing College Vocabulary & Spelling Skills

I.)   Use context to arrive at meaning. Complete the following sentences with words that are familiar to you and that make sense in each sentence. You may write more than one word choice for each blank space. <u>Do not</u> look at or study the new words yet. Answers will vary and your instructor will discuss them with you.

1. Dennis decided to become a lawyer so he could be a(n) ___advocate___ for justice.
2. Some criminals are ___authoritarian___, as proven by their repeated offences, and need to stay locked in prison for life.
3. Frustrations sometimes ___desegregation___ violence.
4. Lenin was a very ___violent___ ruler who ruled with an iron fist.
5. The immigration service checked to see if the man had a ___excruciating___ reason for being in the United States.
6. Ken ___incorrigible___ the statement which he considered to be untrue.
7. In the 1950's, ___legitimate___ began and school children were transported to distant schools in an effort to provide equality in education.
8. A century seems like a long time, yet a ___millennium___ is ten times as long!
9. Our country once had enforced separation of people according to their skin color and that was called ___obnoxious___
10. It has been ___paradoxical___ since the 1960's that most people in this country can get along.
11. There always seems to be a few ___precipitate___ persons who try to ruin good times with their rude behavior.
12. Movie theaters once used ___repudiate___ advertising by flashing a few frames of an advertisement on the screen.
13. The pain from a burst appendix is ___segregation___.
14. Statements that seem to contradict one another, yet may be true, are labeled as being ___subliminal___.
15. There was no ___substantive___ reason for the fall of the stock prices; it seemed to be the nervousness of the brokers that created the decline.

II.)   ***Study the words and definitions below.*** These words and definitions are also on the enclosed CD Rom and may be printed out as study cards. The words are broken into letter groupings for easier spelling. Also, that is followed by a common definition, and common forms of the word that you might encounter. Your instructor will pronounce the words for you or you may want to use an audio dictionary for more help.

1. **advocate** (ad/vo/cate) a lawyer, one who pleads another's case, helper, champion, proponent, defender.
2. **authoritarian** (au/thor/i/tar/ian) absolute ruler, tyrant, despot, dictator, oppressor.
3. **desegregation** (de/seg/re/ga/tion) elimination of segregation or separation of races or ethnic groups; unification, integration.
4. **evidenced** (ev/i/den/ced) outward sign; proven, supported, rationale, reasons.
5. **excruciating** (ex/cru/cia/ting) painful, agonizing, intense, tortuous.
6. **incorrigible** (in/corr/i/gi/ble) not able to be reformed, unredeemable, unrepentant, hardened.
7. **legitimate** (le/gi/ti/mate) lawful, legal, proper, valid, constitutional.
8. **millennium** (mill/enn/i/um) a one thousand year period, a thousand year reign of Jesus Christ as prophesied in the Bible; a thousandth anniversary.
9. **obnoxious** (ob/nox/ious) objectionable, rude, crude, bad-mannered, coarse, disrespectful.
10. **paradoxical** (par/a/dox/i/cal) a statement that seems contradictory yet may be true; brainteaser, dilemma, enigma, riddle, puzzle. Also: **paradox.**
11. **precipitate** (pre/cip/i/tate) to precede the effect and be labeled as the cause whether the event actually was the cause or not, cause, preceding event; to suddenly bring about an event, initiate.
12. **repudiate** (re/pud/ia/te) refuse to recognize, reject as invalid or untrue, disown, disavow, disaffirm, renounce, negate.
13. **segregation** (seg/re/ga/tion) setting apart of races; separation, exclusion, apartheid, isolation.
14. **subliminal** (sub/lim/i/nal) lying below the surface of the conscious perception but still able to produce an effect or create an influence; latent, underlying, subconscious. Also: **subliminally.**
15. **substantive** (sub/stan/tive) considerable, significant, real, independent, self-sufficient.

III.) *Match the words with their definitions.* Draw a line connecting each word with its correct definition.

1. advocate
2. authoritarian
3. desegregation
4. evidenced
5. excruciating
6. incorrigible
7. legitimate
8. millennium
9. obnoxious
10. paradoxical
11. precipitate
12. repudiate
13. segregation
14. subliminal
15. substantive

a. bad-mannered
b. significant
c. separation
d. enigma
e. valid
f. lying below the surface
g. agonizing
h. unredeemable
i. supported
j. one thousand years
k. unification
l. helper
m. dictator
n. reject as invalid
o. to precede

IV.) *Puzzle work.* Now try the interactive puzzle. Put the CD (that came with your workbook) into the computer, and work the puzzle. A paper copy of the puzzle is also included at the end of this chapter.

V.)   Write the correct new word in each sentence below:

substantive	excruciating	paradoxical	evidenced	obnoxious
segregation	millennium	desegregation	authoritarian	legitimate
repudiate	advocate	precipitate	incorrigible	subliminal

1. Dennis decided to become a lawyer so he could be a(n) ___advocate___ for justice.
2. Some criminals are ___authoritarian___, as proven by their repeated offences, and need to stay locked in prison for life.
3. Frustrations sometimes ___desegregation___ violence.
4. Lenin was a very ___evidenced___ ruler who ruled with an iron fist.
5. The immigration service checked to see if the man had a ___excruciating___ reason for being in the United States.
6. Ken ___incorrigible___ the statement which he considered to be untrue.
7. In the 1950's, ___legitimate___ began and school children were transported to distant schools in an effort to provide equality in education.
8. A century seems like a long time, yet a ___millennium___ is ten times as long!
9. Our country once had enforced separation of people according to their skin color and that was called ___obnoxious___.
10. It has been ___paradoxical___ since the 1960's that most people in this country can get along.
11. There always seems to be a few ___precipitate___ persons who try to ruin good times with their rude behavior.
12. Movie theaters once used ___repudiate___ advertising by flashing a few frames of an advertisement on the screen. Although not perceived consciously, many persons found themselves wanting to buy that product.
13. The pain from a burst appendix is ___segregation___.
14. Statements that seem to contradict one another, yet may be true, are labeled as being ___subliminal___.
15. There was no ___substantive___ reason for the fall of the stock prices; it seemed to be the nervousness of the brokers that created the decline.

VI.) Are you ready to take the practice test? You may take the practice test as many times as you want to. Simply insert the CD that came with book into your computer, go to "My Computer", open the CD by clicking on it, find the Practice test folder, choose this chapter's practice test and begin. (You will need a sheet of paper to write your answers on.) When finished, turn back to this chapter and correct your test. The answers are in the same order as exercise II.

VII.) Write a sentence for each new word. Are you ready to use the new words? Write a sentence for each new word.

substantive	excruciating	paradoxical	evidenced	obnoxious
segregation	millennium	desegregation	authoritarian	legitimate
repudiate	advocate	precipitate	incorrigible	subliminal

1. _____
2. _____
3. _____
4. _____
5. _____
6. _____
7. _____
8. _____
9. _____
10. _____
11. _____
12. _____
13. _____
14. _____
15. _____

VIII.) Your instructor may ask you to do the puzzle on the next page. It is the same as the one on your CD. You are able to do it here once or on the CD as many times as you'd like.

Across

1. A statement that seems contradictory yet may be true; brainteaser, dilemma, enigma, riddle, puzzle.

9. A one thousand year period, a thousand year reign of Jesus Christ as prophesied in the Bible; a thousandth anniversary.

10. Elimination of segregation or separation of races or ethic groups; unification, integration.

11. Lawful, legal, proper, valid, constitutional

Down

2. Refuse to recognize, reject as invalid or untrue, disown, disavow, disaffirm, renounce, negate.

3. Objectionable, rude, crude, bad-mannered, coarse, disrespectful.

4. Absolute ruler, tyrant, despot, dictator, oppressor.

5. Not able to reform, unredeemable, unrepentant, hardened.

6. To bring about an event.

7. Considerable, significant, real, independent, self-sufficient

8. Lying below the surface of the conscious perception but still able to produce an effect or create an influence; latent, underlying, subconscious.

Rewrite your words/Practice Test

New word:		Practice writing the new word:		

Rewrite your words/Practice test

New word:		Practice writing the new word:	

Advancing College Vocabulary & Spelling Skills

I.)   Use context to arrive at meaning. Complete the following sentences with words that are familiar to you and that make sense in each sentence. You may write more than one word choice for each blank space. <u>Do not</u> look at or study the new words yet. Answers will vary and your instructor will discuss them with you.

1. In medieval times, armies would ___catapult___ diseased bodies over the fortress wall in an effort to spread disease and defeat the enemy.
2. His opinions are ___complacent___; we just can't get him to any other point of view.
3. Tony is such a(n) ___discontent___; he always expects the worst to happen.
4. Many people are ___emulate___ and do not try to advance in their careers.
5. Martin Luther King Jr. claimed that all of humanity has a(n) ___extremist___ bond that makes us interdependent on one another for our well-being.
6. The demonstrators were charged with ___inexorable___ because they had thrown rocks and bottles at the police.
7. Much ___inextricab___ spread through the population as unemployment became worse.
8. Herod the king was accused of ___infanticide___ because he ordered the killing of all male children less than two years of age.
9. The instructor decided to ___languished___ his previous instructions for the benefit of those who were absent.
10. A form of praise is when some ___optimist___ your actions with similar actions of their own.
11. Many of the prisoners ___pessimist___ in jails that were filthy.
12. Most people are satisfied with the ___provocative___ because change makes them feel insecure.
13. Many great leaders were labeled as ___reiterate___ because they moved societies forward – often against that society's will.
14. Luis is a(n) ___status quo___ because he always thinks that good will come out of every situation.
15. Godiva Chocolates are so ___sublime___, and so expensive too.

II.) *Study the words and definitions below.* These words and definitions are also on the enclosed CD Rom and may be printed out as study cards. The words are broken into letter groupings for easier spelling. Also, that is followed by a common definition, and common forms of the word that you might encounter. Your instructor will pronounce the words for you or you may want to use an audio dictionary for more help.

1. **catapult** (cat/a/pult) launch with great force, toss, shoot, throw. Also: **catapulted.**
2. **complacent** (com/pla/cent) self-satisfied, overly contented.
3. **discontent** (dis/con/tent) dissatisfaction, unhappiness, frustration. Also: **discontentment, discontented.**
4. **emulate** (em/u/late) imitate, equal, excel, surpass. Also: **emulated, emulating, emulates, emulation.**
5. **extremist** (ex/tre/mist) one who goes beyond the norm, one who goes to the extreme; fanatic, rebel, revolutionary, terrorist, militant. Also: **extremism, extremists.**
6. **inexorable** (in/ex/or/able) unresponsive, unimpressionable, immovable, closed minded, unyielding.
7. **inextricable** (in/ex/tri/ca/ble) inescapable, permanently bound together. Also: inextricably, inextricability.
8. **infanticide** (in/fan/ti/cide) infant killing.
9. **languished** (lan/gui/sh/ed) exhausted, depleted, wasted away, deteriorated, weakened. Also: **languish, languishing, languishes.**
10. **optimist** (op/ti/mist) a person who usually expects the best to happen, expecting a favorable future or outcome. Also: **optimistic.**
11. **pessimist** (pess/i/mist) a person who usually expects the worst to happen. Also: **pessimistic, pessimism.**
12. **provocation** (pro/vo/ca/tion) incitement, instigation, stimulant, agitation.
13. **reiterate** (re/i/ter/ate) to repeat, restate, elaborate upon. Also: **reiteration, reiterator.**
14. **status quo** (sta/tus quo) as it is at this time, existing conditions.
15. **sublime** (sub/lime) majestic, supreme, noble, impressive, awe inspiring.

III.) *Match the words with their definitions.* Draw a line connecting each word with its correct definition.

1. catapult
2. complacent
3. discontent
4. emulate
5. extremist
6. inexorable
7. inextricable
8. infanticide
9. languished
10. optimist
11. pessimist
12. provocation
13. reiterate
14. status quo
15. sublime

a. expecting the worst
b. expecting the best
c. majestic
d. unyielding
e. repeat
f. agitation
g. fanatic
h. permanently bound
i. imitate
j. existing conditions
k. unhappiness
l. self-satisfied
m. infant killing
n. wasted away
o. launch with great force

IV.) *Puzzle work.* Now try the interactive puzzle. Put the CD (that came with your workbook) into the computer, and work the puzzle. A paper copy of the puzzle is also included at the end of this chapter.

V.)   Write the correct new word in each sentence below:

inexorable	pessimist	complacent	provocation	catapult
inextricable	discontent	reiterate	infanticide	emulate
extremists	sublime	optimist	languished	status quo

1. In medieval times, armies would ___*catapult*___ diseased bodies over the fortress wall in an effort to spread disease and defeat the enemy.
2. His opinions are ___*complacent*___; we just can't get him to any other point of view.
3. Tony is such a ___*discontent*___; he always expects the worst to happen.
4. Many people are ___*emulate*___ and do not try to advance in their careers.
5. Martin Luther King Jr. claimed that all of humanity has a(n) ___*extremist*___ bond that makes us interdependent on one another for our well-being.
6. The demonstrators were charged with ___*inexorable*___ because they had thrown rocks and bottles at the police.
7. Much ___*inextricable*___ spread through the population as unemployment became worse.
8. Herod the king was accused of ___*infanticide*___ because he ordered the killing of all male children less than two years of age.
9. The instructor decided to ___*languished*___ his previous instructions for the benefit of those who were absent.
10. A form of praise is when some ___*optimist*___ your actions with similar actions of their own.
11. Many of the prisoners ___*pessimist*___ in jails that were filthy.
12. Most people are satisfied with the ___*provocation*___ because change makes them feel insecure.
13. Many great leaders were labeled as ___*reiterate*___ because they moved societies forward – often against that society's will.
14. Luis is a(n) ___*status quo*___ because he always thinks that good will come out of every situation.
15. Godiva Chocolates are so ___*sublime*___, and so expensive too.

VI.) Are you ready to take the practice test? You may take the practice test as many times as you want to. Simply insert the CD that came with book into your computer, go to "My Computer", open the CD by clicking on it, find the Practice test folder, choose this chapter's practice test and begin. (You will need a sheet of paper to write your answers on.) When finished, turn back to this chapter and correct your test. The answers are in the same order as exercise II.

VII.) Write a sentence for each new word. Are you ready to use the new words? Write a sentence for each new word.

inexorable	pessimist	complacent	provocation	catapult
inextricable	discontent	reiterate	infanticide	emulate
extremists	sublime	optimist	languished	status quo

1. _____
2. _____
3. _____
4. _____
5. _____
6. _____
7. _____
8. _____
9. _____
10. _____
11. _____
12. _____
13. _____
14. _____
15. _____

VIII.) Your instructor may ask you to do the puzzle on the next page. It is the same as the one on your CD. You are able to do it here once or on the CD as many times as you'd like.

Across

7. A person who usually expects the best to happen, expecting a favorable future or outcome.

9. Inescapable, permanently bound together.

10. Dissatisfaction, unhappiness, frustration.

11. Launch with great force, toss, shoot, throw.

12. Killing of infants

Down

1. Unresponsive, unimpressionable, immovable, closed minded, unyielding

2. Incitement, instigation, stimulant, agitation.

3. A person who usually expects the worst to happen.

4. Majestic, supreme, noble, impressive, awe inspiring.

5. Self-satisfied, overly contented

6. As it is at this time, existing conditions.

8. To repeat, restate, elaborate upon.

Rewrite your words/Practice Test

New word:		Practice writing the new word:	

Rewrite your words/Practice test

New word:	Practice writing the new word:		

Advancing College Vocabulary & Spelling Skills

I.)   Use context to arrive at meaning. Complete the following sentences with words that are familiar to you and that make sense in each sentence. You may write more than one word choice for each blank space. <u>Do not</u> look at or study the new words yet. Answers will vary and your instructor will discuss them with you.

1.   I wish to ___*appere*___ my earlier statement by adding that I may run for President.
2.   Some evil men have used the technique of ___*pleatfue*___ to accomplish their goals over several decades.
3.   A ___*converse*___ is a person who hates most of humanity.
4.   The devotees claimed that they had a ___*devous*___ vision.
5.   The Congress proposed ___*disubused*___ policies that would have united many diverse communities.
6.   The ___*gradwhsm*___ of the new law had the effect of surprising and saddening its supporters.
7.   The President wanted to ___*integrwhonist*___ with the representatives of the Senate.
8.   Sometimes it's better not to ___*interpose*___ our ideas when they clearly will not be accepted.
9.   Sometimes intellectual ___*jurgon*___ comes from unlikely sources such as small children.
10. Many accused Richard Nixon of being a ___*Mcnacles*___ character who was more concerned with remaining president than telling the truth.
11. Computer technicians have a ___*misanthorpe*___ that is sometimes difficult to understand.
12. The bank received a ___*nullifiation*___ note from the tenant saying that they would have their rent by the 12th of the month.
13. Some people would benefit if they were ___*profundhy*___ from their illusions about life, rather than living their life in a big delusion to later discover that they had wasted it.
14. The prisoners were kept in ___*premissory*___ until they arrived at the prison.
15. Stars have a ___*scintillating*___ beauty about them as they flicker high above us.

II.)   *Study the words and definitions below.* These words and definitions are also on the enclosed CD Rom and may be printed out as study cards. The words are broken into letter groupings for easier spelling. Also, that is followed by a common definition, and common forms of the word that you might encounter. Your instructor will pronounce the words for you or you may want to use an audio dictionary for more help.

1. **append** (app/end) to add to, to supplement, to join to, to unite. Also: **appended, appending, appends, appendage, appendix.**
2. **beatific** (bea/ti/fic) angelic, holy, sanctified, saintly.
3. **converse** (con/ver/se) to exchange thoughts through conversation, to associate, interact, correspond. Also: **conversation, conversed, conversing.**
4. **devious** (de/vi/ous) deceitful, manipulative, tricky, underhanded, treacherous, shifty.
5. **disabused** (dis/ab/used) freed from misconception or falsehood. Also: **disabuse, disabusing.**
6. **gradualism** (grad/ual/ism) advancing toward a goal by gradual stages. Also **gradualist.**
7. **integrationist** (in/te/gra/tion/ist) a person who works for social integration.
8. **interpose** (in/ter/pose) to interject, to come between, to exert authority or influence, to intervene. Also: **interposition, interposed, interposing.**
9. **jargon** (jar/gon) specialized or technical language; double-talk.
10. **manacles** (man/a/cles) restraints; handcuffs, chains, bindings. Also: **manacled, manacle, manacling.**
11. **misanthrope** (mis/an/th/rope) a person that hates mankind, cynic, pessimist, skeptic, scoffer. Also: **misanthropist.**
12. **nullification** (null/i/fi/ca/tion) action of nullifying, canceling, making ineffective, annulling.
13. **profundity** (pro/fun/dity) intellectual depth.
14. **promissory** (prom/iss/ory) carrying a promise.
15. **scintillating** (scin/till/a/ting) shining, sparkling, brightly flickering, twinkling.

III.) *Match the words with their definitions.* Draw a line connecting each word with its correct definition.

1. append
2. beatific
3. converse
4. devious
5. disabused
6. gradualism
7. integrationist
8. interpose
9. jargon
10. manacles
11. misanthrope
12. nullification
13. profundity
14. promissory
15. scintillating

a. one who works for integration
b. to intervene
c. twinkling
d. advancing by gradual stages
e. technical language
f. chains
g. to add to
h. correspond
i. a person who hates mankind
j. freed from misconception
k. saintly
l. deceitful
m. canceling
n. carrying a promise
o. intellectual depth

IV.) *Puzzle work.* Now try the interactive puzzle. Put the CD (that came with your workbook) into the computer, and work the puzzle. A paper copy of the puzzle is also included at the end of this chapter.

V.) Write the correct new word in each sentence below:

converse	beatific	append	devious	gradualism
disabused	jargon	integrationist	interpose	promissory
misanthrope	nullification	manacles	profundity	scintillating

1. I wish to ___*append*___ my earlier statement by adding that I may run for President.
2. Some evil men have used the technique of ___*beatific*___ to accomplish their goals over several decades.
3. A ___*converse*___ is a person who hates most of humanity.
4. The devotees claimed that they had a ___*devious*___ vision.
5. The Congress proposed ___*disabused*___ policies that would have united many diverse communities.
6. The ___*gradualism*___ of the new law had the effect of surprising and saddening its supporters.
7. The President wanted to ___*integrationist*___ with the representatives of the Senate.
8. Sometimes it's better not to ___*interpose*___ our ideas when they clearly will not be accepted.
9. Sometimes intellectual ___*jargon*___ comes from unlikely sources such as small children.
10. Many accused Richard Nixon of being a ___*manacles*___ character who was more concerned with remaining president than telling the truth.
11. Computer technicians have a ___*misanthrope*___ that is sometimes difficult to understand.
12. The bank received a ___*nullification*___ note from the tenant saying that they would have their rent by the 12th of the month.
13. Some people would benefit if they were ___*profundity*___ from their illusions about life, rather than living their life in a big delusion to later discover that they had wasted it.
14. The prisoners were kept in ___*promissory*___ until they arrived at the prison.
15. Stars have a ___*scintillating*___ beauty about them as they flicker high above us.

VI.) Are you ready to take the practice test? You may take the practice test as many times as you want to. Simply insert the CD that came with book into your computer, go to "My Computer", open the CD by clicking on it, find the Practice test folder, choose this chapter's practice test and begin. (You will need a sheet of paper to write your answers on.) When finished, turn back to this chapter and correct your test. The answers are in the same order as exercise II.

VII.) Write a sentence for each new word. Are you ready to use the new words? Write a sentence for each new word.

converse	beatific	append	devious	gradualism
disabused	jargon	integrationist	interpose	promissory
misanthrope	nullification	manacles	profundity	scintillating

1. _____
2. _____
3. _____
4. _____
5. _____
6. _____
7. _____
8. _____
9. _____
10. _____
11. _____
12. _____
13. _____
14. _____
15. _____

VIII.) Your instructor may ask you to do the puzzle on the next page. It is the same as the one on your CD. You are able to do it here once or on the CD as many times as you'd like.

Across

2. Advancing toward a goal by gradual stages.

4. To add to, to supplement, to join to, to unite.

6. Specialized or technical language; double-talk.

10. To interject, to come between, to exert authority or influence, to intervene.

11. A person who works for social integration.

12. Deceitful, manipulative, tricky, underhanded, treacherous, shifty.

Down

1. Shining, sparkling, brightly flickering, twinkling.

3. Restraints; handcuffs, chains, bindings.

5. Action of nullifying, canceling, making ineffective, annulling

7. Carrying a promise.

8. Intellectual depth

9. To exchange thoughts through conversation, to associate, interact, correspond.

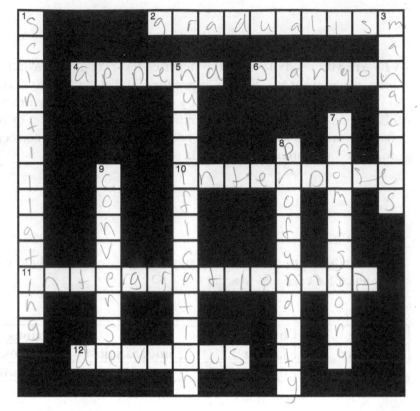

Rewrite your words/Practice Test

New word: **Practice writing the new word:**

Rewrite your words/Practice test

New word:		Practice writing the new word:		

Advancing College Vocabulary & Spelling Skills

I.) Use context to arrive at meaning. Complete the following sentences with words that are familiar to you and that make sense in each sentence. You may write more than one word choice for each blank space. <u>Do not</u> look at or study the new words yet. Answers will vary and your instructor will discuss them with you.

1. Most religions consider it a serious offence to ___blasphere___ the name of God.
2. The ___cleaving___ that were passed into law benefited the order in society.
3. Some rulers know that by actions of ___confiention___ they can receive the popular vote since people rarely turn down gifts and usually will not harm the giver.
4. Some people are found ___destitute___ to their mistaken ideas long after the general population has rejected those ideas.
5. None of us possess ___dispassionate___ from deception; we must all use our knowledge wisely.
6. Until the early 1900's, United States citizens did not have an income tax ___edicts___.
7. Income taxes create ___Immunity___ between the rich and the poor.
8. Thomas Jefferson left a(n) ___indelible___ mark on history through his writing of the Declaration of Independence.
9. People with too much time on their hands often become ___insufferable___.
10. The old man was unable to work and became ___instigate___.
11. Why do many teenagers seem to have ___largesse___ appetites?
12. Once independence was declared, the course of events seemed ___liability___.
13. A judge should have a(n) ___unmeddlesome___ character so that every person receives a fair trial.
14. The prisoners were separated so that no one would be able to ___unalterable___ trouble.
15. Cigarettes were ___unprocurable___ in many of the out lying island communities.

II.) *Study the words and definitions below.* These words and definitions are also on the enclosed CD Rom and may be printed out as study cards. The words are broken into letter groupings for easier spelling. Also, that is followed by a common definition, and common forms of the word that you might encounter. Your instructor will pronounce the words for you or you may want to use an audio dictionary for more help.

1. **blaspheme** (blas/ph/eme) verbally profane, speak irreverently of God or other sacred personage, swear, curse, cuss, desecrate. Also: **blasphemy, blasphemed, blaspheming, blasphemous.**
2. **cleaving** (clea/ving) hanging on, faithfulness, cling, stick to. Also can mean: cutting, separating, splitting.
3. **contention** (con/ten/tion) discord, antagonism, disharmony, strife, conflict.
4. **destitute** (des/ti/tute) penniless, broke, impoverished, poor. Also: **destitution.**
5. **dispassionate** (dis/pass/ion/ate) impartial, unbiased, fair, just, unaffected by passion. Also: **dispassionately.**
6. **edicts** (e/dicts) formal pronouncement, proclamation, decree, directive, command.
7. **immunity** (imm/un/ity) exemption from law; resistance to disease; imperviousness, endurance.
8. **indelible** (in/del/ible) permanent, unable to remove.
9. **insatiable** (in/sa/tia/ble) impossible to satisfy, rapacious, gluttonous, voracious. Also: **insatiability, insatiably**.
10. **instigate** (in/sti/ga/te) to stir up, to incite, ferment.
11. **largesse** (lar/gesse) (or largess) liberal bestowing of gifts, bestowing of gifts in a condescending manner.
12. **liability** (lia/bil/ity) an obligation, debt; also vulnerability, susceptibility.
13. **meddlesome** (medd/le/some) interfering, intrusive, snoopy.
14. **unalterable** (un/al/ter/able) not able to change, unreformable, unredeemable, incorrigible, unrepentant.
15. **unprocurable** (un/pro/cur/able) not able to acquire, unobtainable.

III.) *Match the words with their definitions.* Draw a line connecting each word with its correct definition.

1. blaspheme
2. cleaving
3. contention
4. destitute
5. dispassionate
6. edicts
7. immunity
8. indelible
9. insatiable
10. instigate
11. largesse
12. liability
13. meddlesome
14. unalterable
15. unprocurable

a. debt
b. permanent
c. proclamation
d. unobtainable
e. resistance to disease
f. desecrate
g. discord, strife
h. impossible to satisfy
i. clinging
j. incite
k. obligation
l. liberal bestowing of gifts
m. intrusive
n. not able to change
o. unaffected

IV.) *Puzzle work.* Now try the interactive puzzle. Put the CD (that came with your workbook) into the computer, and work the puzzle. A paper copy of the puzzle is also included at the end of this chapter.

V.)   Write the correct new word in each sentence below:

largesse	immunity	contention	destitute	dispassionate
insatiable	unprocurable	unalterable	blaspheme	edicts
liability	meddlesome	cleaving	indelible	instigate

1. Most religions consider it a serious offence to ___blaspheme___ the name of God.
2. The ___cleaving___ that were passed into law benefited the order in society.
3. Some rulers know that by actions of ___contention___ they can receive the popular vote since people rarely turn down gifts and usually will not harm the giver.
4. Some people are found ___destitute___ to their mistaken ideas long after the general population has rejected those ideas.
5. None of us possess ___dispassionate___ from deception; we must all use our knowledge wisely.
6. Until the early 1900's, United States citizens did not have an income tax ___edicts___.
7. Income taxes create ___immunity___ between the rich and the poor.
8. Thomas Jefferson left a(n) ___indelible___ mark on history through his writing of the Declaration of Independence.
9. People with too much time on their hands often become ___insatiable___.
10. The old man was unable to work and became ___instigate___.
11. Why do many teenagers seem to have ___largesse___ appetites?
12. Once independence was declared, the course of events seemed ___liability___.
13. A judge should have a(n) ___meddlesome___ character so that every person receives a fair trial.
14. The prisoners were separated so that no one would be able to ___instigate___ trouble.
15. Cigarettes were ___unprocurable___ in many of the out lying island communities.

VI.) Are you ready to take the practice test? You may take the practice test as many times as you want to. Simply insert the CD that came with book into your computer, go to "My Computer", open the CD by clicking on it, find the Practice test folder, choose this chapter's practice test and begin. (You will need a sheet of paper to write your answers on.) When finished, turn back to this chapter and correct your test. The answers are in the same order as exercise II.

VII.) Write a sentence for each new word. Are you ready to use the new words? Write a sentence for each new word.

largesse	immunity	contention	destitute	dispassionate
insatiable	unprocurable	unalterable	blaspheme	edicts
liability	meddlesome	cleaving	indelible	instigate

1. _____
2. _____
3. _____
4. _____
5. _____
6. _____
7. _____
8. _____
9. _____
10. _____
11. _____
12. _____
13. _____
14. _____
15. _____

VIII.) Your instructor may ask you to do the puzzle on the next page. It is the same as the one on your CD. You are able to do it here once or on the CD as many times as you'd like.

Across

1. Formal pronouncement, proclamation, decree, directive, command.

4. Impartial, unbiased, fair, just, unaffected by passion.

6. Permanent, unable to remove.

9. Not able to change, unredeemable, incorrigible, unrepentant.

10. Discord, antagonism, disharmony, strife, conflict.

11. Hanging on, faithfulness, cling, stick to. Also can mean, separating, splitting

Down

2. Impossible to satisfy, rapacious, gluttonous voracious.

3. To stir up, to incite, ferment.

4. Penniless, broke, impoverished, poor.

5. Interfering, intrusive, snoopy.

7. An obligation, dept; also vulnerability, susceptibility.

8. Exemption from law; resistance to disease; imperviousness, endurance.

Rewrite your words/Practice Test

New word:		Practice writing the new word:		

Rewrite your words/Practice test

New word: **Practice writing the new word:**

Advancing College Vocabulary & Spelling Skills

I.) Use context to arrive at meaning. Complete the following sentences with words that are familiar to you and that make sense in each sentence. You may write more than one word choice for each blank space. <u>Do not</u> look at or study the new words yet. Answers will vary and your instructor will discuss them with you.

1. The ___*Clyasevent*___ of the Captain led to his new ranking of Private 1st class.
2. The officer asked the drunken man to ___*all harony*___.
3. Evil persons are often labeled as workers of ___*averse*___.
4. Jessica is a faithful ___*re serye*___ to the Democratic Party.
5. Tabitha's ___*chstre*___ on civil rights was well received by all who heard her.
6. One million dollars is a(n) ___*cleshst*___ amount of money.
7. Ronald Reagan said he was ___*disvourst*___ to eating broccoli.
8. There is so much ___*dissensun*___ between the Palestinians and the Jews in the Middle East!
9. Both political groups keep ___*qveluny*___ on the other's rights.
10. The troops had to ___*hyproevte*___ the town to force the enemy to surrender.
11. It was a(n) ___*Imqunty*___ fight that lasted four days and saw many casualties.
12. Such ___*prechyums*___ was everywhere as the victim's bodies were pulled from the Twin Towers.
13. The Mayor began to ___*hvreqns0rl*___ the leaders of many countries for not speaking out against the human rights abuses.
14. The leader of France was labeled a(n) ___*denvard*___ because he said that he wanted peace, but later he was accused of aiding the enemy in their escapes.
15. Even though Bill Clinton seemed to have committed many serious offences, he also seemed ___*unimpcenhrlu*___ as Congress fought over whether to impeach him or not.

II.) ***Study the words and definitions below.*** These words and definitions are also on the enclosed CD Rom and may be printed out as study cards. The words are broken into letter groupings for easier spelling. Also, that is followed by a common definition, and common forms of the word that you might encounter. Your instructor will pronounce the words for you or you may want to use an audio dictionary for more help.

1. **abasement** (a/base/ment) to lower in rank, humble, deflate, humiliate. Also: **abase, abased, abasing, abases.**
2. **adherent** (ad/her/ent) supporter, enthusiast, disciple, zealot, fan, follower.
3. **averse** (a/ver/se) opposed to, distaste for, adversarial, opposing, unfriendly, hostile, antagonistic. Also: **aversely.**
4. **besiege** (be/sie/ge) surround with hostile forces, all encompassing attack, assault, storm, beset, encircle, siege. Also: **besieged, besieging.**
5. **chastise** (chas/tise) rebuke, criticize severely, discipline, castigate, correct. Also: **chastisement, chastised, chastising, chastises.**
6. **desist** (de/sist) to cease, to end, halt, terminate, discontinue, suspend. Also: **desisted, desists, desisting**
7. **discourse** (dis/cour/se) conversation, communication, dissertation, oration, exposition. Also: **discourses, discoursing, discoursed.**
8. **dissension** (diss/en/sion) disagreement, antagonism, friction, contention, discordance, strife, disunity, difference, variance.
9. **grueling** (grue/ling) very physically or mentally demanding.
10. **hypocrite** (hy/po/crite) a person who claims to be something that they are not, sham, phony, insincere person. Also: **hypocrisy, hypocrisies, hypocritical.**
11. **iniquity** (in/i/quity) wickedness, barbarous, possessing inhuman qualities, savagery, gross immorality. Also: **iniquities.**
12. **prodigious** (pro/di/gious) huge, enormous, extraordinary, marvelous.
13. **transgressing** (trans/gress/ing) going beyond proper limits, overstepping, violating. Also: **transgressor, transgression, transgressed, transgresses, transgress.**
14. **travail** (tra/vail) exhausting and difficult labor; childbirth; tribulation, agony, hard work. Also: **travailing, travailed, travails.**
15. **unimpeachable** (un/im/peach/able) Not able to impeach, not able to remove; beyond doubt, unquestionable.

III.) *Match the words with their definitions.* Draw a line connecting each word with its correct definition.

1. abasement	a. insincere person
2. adherent	b. beyond doubt
3. averse	c. physically/mentally demanding
4. besiege	d. extraordinary
5. chastise	e. hard work
6. desist	f. gross immorality
7. discourse	g. disagreement
8. dissension	h. conversation
9. grueling	i. humiliation
10. hypocrite	j. follower
11. iniquity	k. discipline
12. prodigious	l. violating
13. transgressing	m. antagonism
14. travail	n. to cease
15. unimpeachable	o. surround with hostile forces

IV.) *Puzzle work.* Now try the interactive puzzle. Put the CD (that came with your workbook) into the computer, and work the puzzle. A paper copy of the puzzle is also included at the end of this chapter.

V.)   Write the correct new word in each sentence below:

unimpeachable	chastise	hypocrite	travail	besiege
grueling	averse	transgressing	dissension	abasement
iniquity	desist	adherent	discourse	prodigious

1. The ___*abasement*___ of the Captain led to his new ranking of Private 1st class.
2. The officer asked the drunken man to ___*adherent*___.
3. Evil persons are often labeled as workers of ___*averse*___.
4. Jessica is a faithful ___*besiege*___ to the Democratic Party.
5. Tabitha's ___*chastise*___ on civil rights was well received by all who heard her.
6. One million dollars is a(n) ___*desist*___ amount of money.
7. Ronald Reagan said he was ___*averse*___ to eating broccoli.
8. There is so much ___*dissension*___ between the Palestinians and the Jews in the Middle East!
9. Both political groups keep ___*grueling*___ on the other's rights.
10. The troops had to ___*hypocrite*___ the town to force the enemy to surrender.
11. It was a(n) ___*iniquity*___ fight that lasted four days and saw many casualties.
12. Such ___*prodigious*___ was everywhere as the victim's bodies were pulled from the Twin Towers.
13. The Mayor began to ___*transgress*___ the leaders of many countries for not speaking out against the human rights abuses.
14. The leader of France was labeled a(n) ___*travail*___ because he said that he wanted peace, but later he was accused of aiding the enemy in their escapes.
15. Even though Bill Clinton seemed to have committed many serious offences, he also seemed ___*unimpeachable*___ as Congress fought over whether to impeach him or not.

VI.) Are you ready to take the practice test? You may take the practice test as many times as you want to. Simply insert the CD that came with book into your computer, go to "My Computer", open the CD by clicking on it, find the Practice test folder, choose this chapter's practice test and begin. (You will need a sheet of paper to write your answers on.) When finished, turn back to this chapter and correct your test. The answers are in the same order as exercise II.

VII.) Write a sentence for each new word. Are you ready to use the new words? Write a sentence for each new word.

unimpeachable	chastise	hypocrite	travail	besiege
grueling	averse	transgressing	dissension	abasement
iniquity	desist	adherent	discourse	prodigious

1. _____
2. _____
3. _____
4. _____
5. _____
6. _____
7. _____
8. _____
9. _____
10. _____
11. _____
12. _____
13. _____
14. _____
15. _____

VIII.) Your instructor may ask you to do the puzzle on the next page. It is the same as the one on your CD. You are able to do it here once or on the CD as many times as you'd like.

Across

1. Supporter, enthusiast, disciple, zealot, fan, follower.

4. Not able to impeach, not able to remove; beyond doubt, unquestionable.

6. Rebuke, criticize severely, discipline, castigate, correct.

8. Exhausting and difficult labor; childbirth; tribulation, agony hard work.

10. Opposed to, distaste for, adversarial, opposing, unfriendly, hostile, antagonistic.

11. To cease, to end, halt, terminate, discontinue, suspend

12. Surround with hostile forces, all encompassing attack, assault, storm, beset, encircle, siege.

13. Huge, enormous, extraordinary, marvelous.

Down

2. A person who claims to be something that they are not, sham, phony, insincere person.

3. Going beyond proper limits, overstepping, violating.

5. To lower in rank, humble, deflate, humiliate.

7. Wickedness, barbarous, possessing in human qualities, savagery, gross immorality.

9. Very physically or mentally demanding

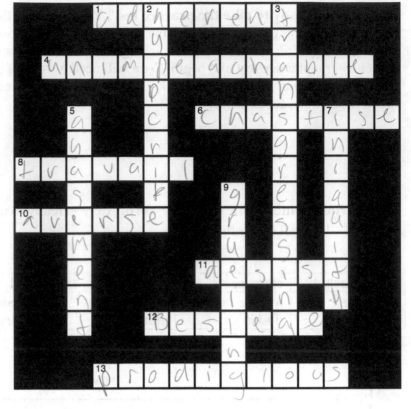

Rewrite your words/Practice Test

New word:		Practice writing the new word:	

Rewrite your words/Practice test

New word:		Practice writing the new word:	

Appendix

Appendix

Using StudyMate Activities on an iPod
(Windows - iTunes 6.0 or higher)

Overview
StudyMate activities created for iPods can be downloaded and then viewed with the iPod's "Photos" function. The iTunes software is used to manage the synchronization of the StudyMate activities with the iPod. Within iTunes, a folder is specified for photo synchronization. When the StudyMate activities are added to this photo folder, the iPod will be able to display the activities the next time it is updated. The general process for copying StudyMate activities to an iPod is as follows:

- Set up an iTunes "Photos" folder (if this hasn't yet been done)
- Download the file containing the iPod version of the StudyMate activities
- Unzip this file and copy the folder to the "Photos" folder set up for use with iTunes
- Update the iPod with iTunes
- From the iPod menu, select the "Photos" option
- Locate the StudyMate activity from the list and view it

Setting Up an iTunes Photos Folder
1) If you haven't already done so, create a folder on your computer for storing photos that will be synchronized with iTunes and your iPod. For example, to create a folder, follow these steps:

- Click **Start** on the Windows desktop
- Select **My Documents**
- From the menu bar in My Documents select **File** > **New** > **Folder**
- Type a folder name like **iTunes Photos** and press Enter.

2) To establish this as the default Photo folder in iTunes, follow these steps:

- Connect the iPod to the computer and select your iPod in the iTunes source list.
- If using iTunes 7.0 or higher, click the **Photos** tab. (If using iTunes 6.0, click the "Options" button [image], select the **iPod** tab, and then select the **Photos** tab from the preferences below.)
- Select the checkbox "Synchronize photos from". From the pull-down list at the right select **Choose Folder...**
- Browse to the photo folder to be used for synchronizing and click **OK**. (If the example above was followed for creating a photo folder, browse to **My Documents**, click once on the folder **iTunes Photos**, and click **OK**.)

    Note: iTunes can't access photos that are stored on a locked volume, like a CD.

- Click Apply and your iPod will be synchronized with the photo folder the

A

next time it is updated. When the update is complete, eject the iPod (CTL+E) and disconnect it from the computer.

Downloading StudyMate Activities from the Web

1) From the web page containing the StudyMate activities, click the download link for the iPod device you plan to use. (The iPod Video uses a 320 x 240 display; the iPod Nano uses 176 x 132).

> Several activities are available for iPod, PSP, etc.
> **Download for iPod Video, Zune, PSP (320x240 pixels)**
> **Download for iPod Nano (176x132 pixels)**
>
> **Download and installation instructions**

2) When the following screen appears, click "Save".

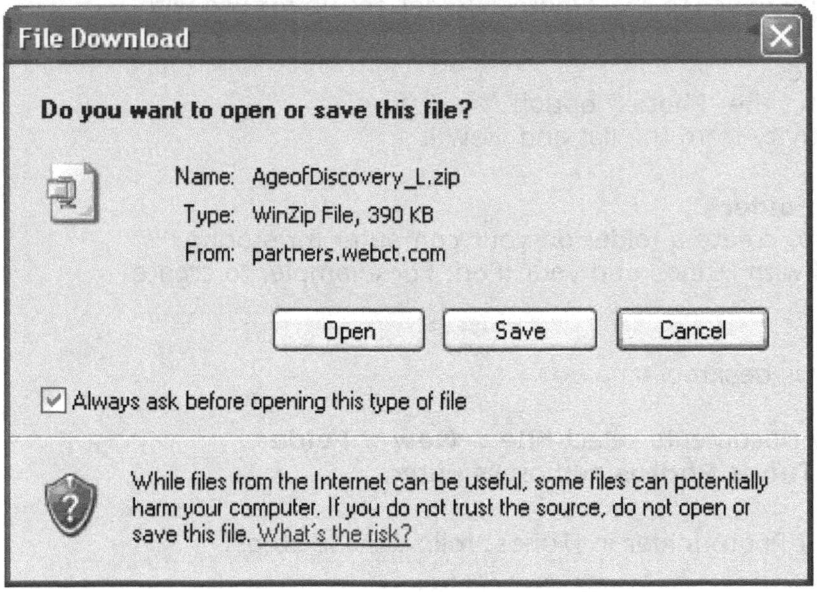

3) The following screen will appear:

Locate the photo folder that is set up to synchronize with iTunes. Click **Save** to download the file to that folder.

5) Use **My Computer** to locate the file that was downloaded. The file is a compressed (zip) archive that must be uncompressed (unzipped) before it can be used. If you have WinZip, unzip the file and keep the unzipped contents in the same folder. If you don't have WinZip, click once on the file name in My Computer, select **File** from the menu bar, select **Open With**, and then click **Compressed (zipped) Folders**.

6) At this point the uncompressed folder should appear. To save hard drive space, you can delete the original .zip file that was downloaded from the web since it is no longer needed.

7) If you have already set up an iTunes photo folder (see above "*Setting Up an iTunes Photos Folder*") then simply update your iPod with iTunes.

Viewing StudyMate Activities on an iPod
Once the iPod has been synchronized with the Photos folder that contains the StudyMate activities, follow these steps to view the activities on the iPod:
1) Start your iPod
2) Select **Photos** from the main menu
3) Select the folder containing the StudyMate materials
4) Scroll forward through each screen to review the materials

Using StudyMate Activities on an iPod
(Macintosh - iTunes 6.0 or higher)

Overview
StudyMate activities created for iPods can be downloaded and then viewed with the iPod's "Photos" function. The iTunes software is used to manage the synchronization of the StudyMate activities with the iPod. Within iTunes, a folder is specified for photo synchronization. When the StudyMate activities are added to this photo folder, the iPod will be able to display the activities the next time it is updated. The general process for copying StudyMate activities to an iPod is as follows:

- Set up an iTunes "Photos" folder (if this hasn't yet been done)
- Download the file containing the iPod version of the StudyMate activities
- Copy the downloaded folder to the "Photos" folder set up for use with iTunes
- Update the iPod with iTunes
- From the iPod menu, select the "Photos" option
- Locate the StudyMate activity from the list and view it

Setting Up an iTunes Photos Folder
1) If you haven't already done so, create a folder on your computer for storing photos that will be synchronized with iTunes and your iPod. For example, to create a folder, follow these steps:

- Go to the **Pictures** folder
- Create a new folder in the Pictures folder using Command+Shift+N (or go to File > New Folder)
- Click on the 'untitled folder' title of the new folder and replace the name with something like **iTunes Photos**

2) To establish this as the default Photo folder in iTunes, follow these steps:

- Connect the iPod to the computer using the cable that came with your iPod
- When the iPod icon appears in the iTunes window, select it and click the **Photos** tab.
- Select the checkbox "Sync photos from". From the pull-down list at the right, select **Choose Folder...**
- Locate the photo folder to be used for synchronizing and click **Choose**. (If the example above was followed for creating a photo folder, locate the **Pictures** folder and choose **iTunes Photos**.)
- Select **All photos** or **Selected folders**, depending on your preference.
- Click **Apply** and your iPod will be synchronized with the photo folder the next time it is updated. When the update is complete, eject the iPod and disconnect it from the computer.

Downloading StudyMate Activities from the Web
1) From the web page containing the StudyMate activities, click the download link for the iPod device you plan to use. (The iPod Video uses a 320 x 240 display; the iPod Nano uses 176 x 132).
2) Once the download is complete, copy the folder to the photo folder that is set up to

synchronize with iTunes (see above "Setting Up an iTunes Photos Folder").
3) Connect the iPod to the computer using the cable that came with your iPod. Then update your iPod with iTunes to complete the synchronization with the photo folder.

Viewing StudyMate Activities on an iPod
Once the iPod has been synchronized with the Photos folder that contains the StudyMate activities, follow these steps to view the activities on the iPod:
1) Start your iPod
2) Select **Photos** from the main menu
3) Select the folder containing the StudyMate materials
4) Scroll forward through each screen to review the materials

Using StudyMate Activities on a Sony PSP
(Windows)

Overview
StudyMate activities created for the PSP can be downloaded and then viewed from the PSP's PHOTO folder. You will need a formatted Memory Stick Duo for your PSP and an USB A to mini-B cable to connect your PSP to your computer. The general process for copying StudyMate activities to a PSP is as follows:

- Ensure that you have the proper equipment for your PSP to download files from your PC (Memory Stick Duo and USB A to mini-B cable to connect your PSP to your computer)
- Format PSP's Memory Stick, and if necessary, install PSP to your PC
- Download the zipped file containing the StudyMate activities to your PSP folder on your PC
- Unzip this file and copy the folder to the PSP's PHOTO folder
- View StudyMate activities on PSP by navigating to your PHOTO folder

Setting up the PSP with Your Computer
If you haven't done so already, follow these steps to set up the PSP with your Windows computer.

1) Check to see if you have a Memory Stick Duo in your PSP by going to **Home** > **Settings**. Scroll to the PSP's **System Settings** and use the PSP's "**x**" button to select this option. Then, scroll to the **Format Memory Stick** and select.

2) To connect your PSP with your PC, follow these steps:

- Hook up the USB cable by connecting one end to the top of the PSP and the other to the PC.
- Turn on the PSP and select the USB Connection under the **Settings** item in the Cross Media bar.
- From the PSP's **Settings** menu, select **USB Connect** (your computer should recognize the newly attached drive).
- You will be prompted by your computer to install the proper PSP drivers. Your computer will need to reboot.
- When your computer reboots, navigate to **My Computer** and look for your newly installed removable disk drive (Generally "G").
- Open the newly found drive by double clicking it.
- By default, there will be four folders in your "G:\PSP" folder (GAME, MUSIC, PHOTO, and SAVEDATA). The PHOTO folder is where you will store your StudyMate activities.

Downloading StudyMate Activities from the Web
1) Connect the PSP to your computer.

2) From the web page containing the StudyMate activities, click the first download link labeled "Download for iPod Video, Zune, or PSP (320x240 pixels)".

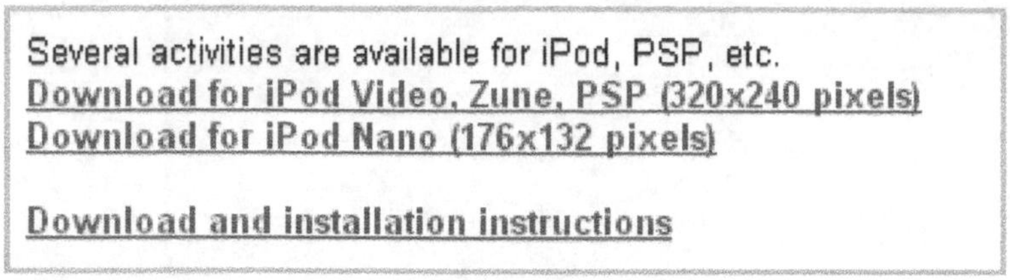

Several activities are available for iPod, PSP, etc.
Download for iPod Video, Zune, PSP (320x240 pixels)
Download for iPod Nano (176x132 pixels)

Download and installation instructions

3) When the following screen appears, click "Save".

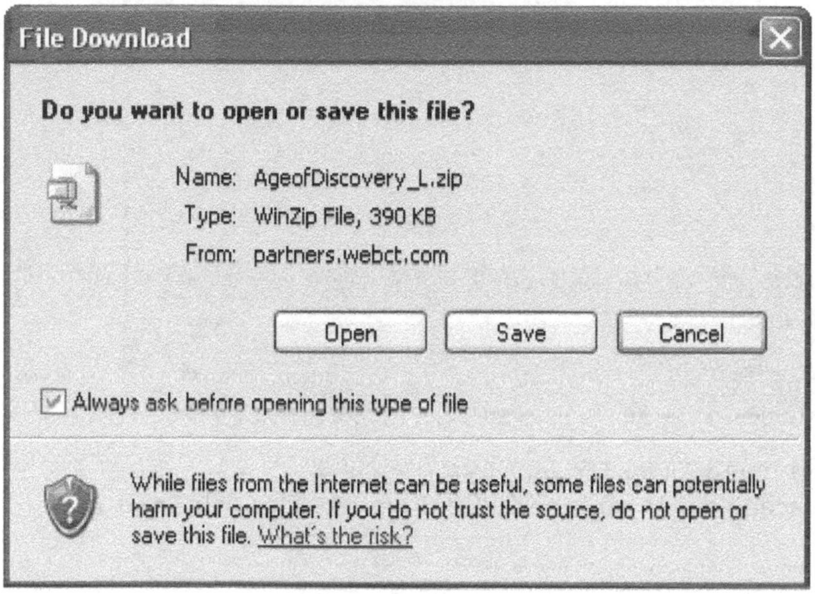

3) The following screen will now appear:

4) Navigate to the new drive and Photo folder for your PSP (Usually G:\PSP\PHOTO where "G" is replaceable with your new PSP drive letter). Click **Save** to download the file to that folder.

5) Use **My Computer** to navigate to the file that was downloaded. The file is a compressed (zip) archive that must be uncompressed (unzipped) before it can be used. If you have WinZip, unzip the file and keep the unzipped contents in the same folder. If you don't have WinZip, click once on the file name in My Computer, select **File** from the menu bar, select **Open With**, and then click **Compressed (zipped) Folders**.

6) At this point the uncompressed folder should appear. To save hard drive space, you can delete the original .zip file that was downloaded from the web since it is no longer needed.

Viewing StudyMate Activities on a PSP
Once the StudyMate files have been added to your PSP's PHOTO folder, they can be viewed in Windows before disconnecting the PSP from your computer. To view the activities from the PSP, disconnect the USB cable and follow these steps:
1) Move to the **PHOTO** folder on your PSP
2) Here you will see the Memory Stick icon and the amount of free space remaining on it
3) Select this by pressing the "**x**" button
4) Select and scroll through the StudyMate activities